NEW JACK CITY
Sport Climbing Guide

by Jordan Robbins

New Jack City Sport Climbing Guide
First Edition (Second Printing)

Copyright 2015 Onsight Media. No part of this book may be reproduced in any way without written permission by the author.

ISBN: 978-0-692-58918-2

Library of Congress Control Number: 2015919818

Photography and Topos: Jordan Robbins
Reviewed by: Jack Marshall, Sam Owings, Geoff Fullerton
Editors: Caitlin Hawekotte, Lauren Robbins

Contact: Jordan@onsightmedia.org
Website: www.onsightmedia.org

Warning and Liability:
Rock climbing is inherently dangerous and anyone participating accepts the potential risks. All information in this book is provided with a best effort and "as is." This book is presented as an approximate guide and not definitive. Always inspect the route and bolts in person and observe current rock conditions. It is the readers responsibility to take all precautions in order to engage in safe climbing.

NEW JACK CITY
Sport Climbing Guide

by Jordan Robbins

Acknowledgements

First, I want to thank my awesome wife (and editor), **Lauren**, for her support, patience, and sacrifice while making this book. My long nights and endless weekends away are what made this book possible. This book exists because of her help and support.

Jack Marshall and Sam Owings, without you, New Jack City would not exist nor would this guidebook. Your support, guidance, and help throughout the development of this book was immense. Thank you for spending weekend after weekend with me reviewing, grading, putting up new routes, and mostly just climbing and having fun. I truly appreciate the time spent together and the friendship that developed. **Catalina and Ryan**, thank you for letting me crash your family time. New Jack City would not be the place it is without your support over the years.

Geoff Fullerton, thank you for spending your time and effort putting up routes in NJC and recently trying to remember the details! I really appreciate your help in getting things accurate.

Kyle Heagle, the best climbing partner I could ask for, thanks for being there and providing support, laughs and friendship. I really appreciate your passion for climbing and all of your help.

Thank you to **Louie Anderson, Troy Mayr, Scott Cosgrove,** and all the developers of NJC.

Thank you to **Randy Vogel, Louie Anderson, Troy Mayr, Brad Singer and Tom Slater** for your awesome and inspiring guidebooks for Southern California climbing.

Thanks to all the climbers I've met at New Jack. Your words of encouragement, conversation, friendliness, and laughs are what makes climbing at NJC so awesome!

Audrey and Henry,
I love you both very much.
I hope we can all use this book together for many years to come.

Table of Contents

Introduction ... 1
- History ... 3
- Geology ... 3
- Flora and Fauna ... 4
- Weather ... 4
- Camping ... 5
- Etiquette ... 7
- Directions ... 9
- Local Resources ... 10
- Topo Legend ... 11
- Necessary Equipment ... 11

Crag Overview ... 15
- Entrance Area Crags ... 18
- The Land That Time Forgot ... 19
- West Canyon Crags ... 19
- East Canyon Crags ... 20

Entrance Area Crags ... 23
- The Cave ... 29
- The Leaning Tower ... 33
- Deadbolt Wall ... 37
- The Critic ... 41
- Intersection Rocks ... 43
- Valentine Wall ... 47
- The Snack Shop ... 50
- White Face ... 52
- White Streak Face ... 57
- Roadside West ... 59
- Roadside Crag ... 61

The Land That Time Forgot ... 67
- Bedrock Wall ... 75
- Bighorn Buttress ... 77
- Hidden Valley ... 83
- Dike Wall ... 99

Table of Contents

West Canyon Crags — 101
- Arch Rock — 107
- Club Butte — 110
- Sunshine Face — 115
- Liz Hurley Boulder — 116
- Predator Wall — 119
- Dude Ranch — 135
- Upper Dude Ranch — 136
- Lower Dude Ranch — 138
- Beyond Dude Ranch — 141
- Toy Block — 142
- Korean Wall — 145
- Cliffs of Insanity — 146
- Scott Cosgrove Memorial Buttress — 148
- Cosgrove Wall — 151
- Hidden Grotto — 152
- The Watchtower — 156
- Fullerton Wall - South — 158

East Canyon Crags — 161
- Parking Lot Rock — 175
- Hidden Wall — 177
- Sunnyside Wall — 179
- Hueco Wall — 183
- The Pinnacle — 189
- Crucified Crag — 193
- Beyond The Crucified — 197
- Indirect Crag — 199
- Raven Rocks — 201
- Raven Rocks East — 203
- Raven Rocks North — 205
- Raven Rocks West — 215
- Raven Rocks South — 221
- Raven Gallery — 227
- The Getaway — 229
- Upper Getaway — 235
- Raven's Roost — 236
- The Shreen — 237

Table of Contents

Nose Wall ... 238
Fantasy Island ... 239
The Fairway ... 243
Hard Rock Cafe ... 249
Slab City ... 251
The Finger ... 253
Prodigy Pile ... 255
Twin Towers ... 257
Pat and Jack Pinnacle ... 263
Lethal Rock ... 267
The Fin ... 271
Crossfire Crag ... 273
Boy Scout Wall ... 281

Routes by Grade ... 289

Index ... 299

Introduction

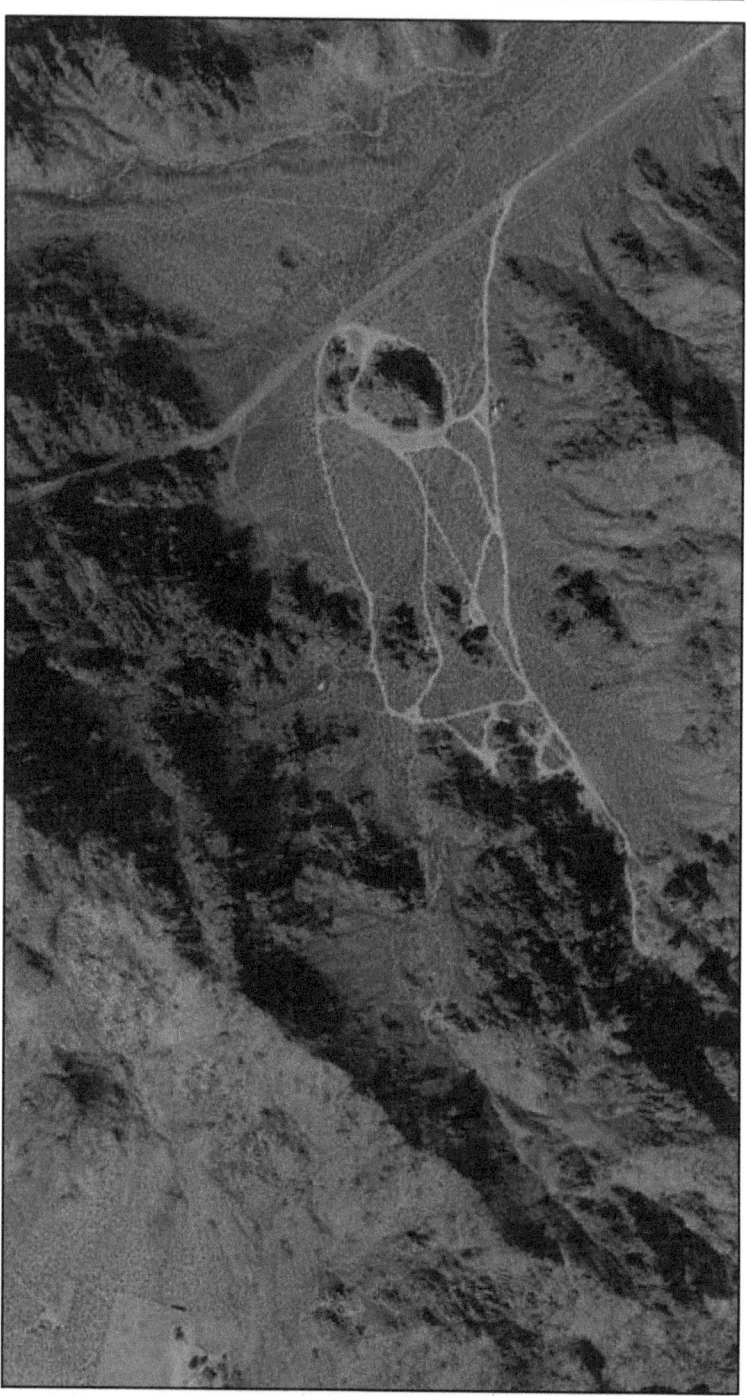

Introduction

History

New Jack City was discovered in the mid-nineties by Jack Marshall and Sam Owings. Over the next 20 years, Jack, Sam, and others, climbed, established, and bolted the approximately 300 routes in New Jack City (NJC). It was converted from a trash dumping ground with burned-out cars to what it is now a cleaned-up, developed campground and legitimized climbing area.

Located between Barstow and Apple Valley, NJC lies in the Traer Agua ("Bring Water") Canyon. Recent popularity and past lawlessness has led to the Bureau of Land Management's developing and maintaining the Sawtooth Canyon Campground.

While some prefer the old ways, it is hard to argue with planned conservation and management in order to keep the area accessible and beautiful. As you walk around, you will notice the attention to detail, such as small fences leading to the nicely groomed trails and belay and spectating benches lining the crags. New Jack City is an easily accessible Southern California sport climbing destination that has something for everyone.

Geology

New Jack City is nestled in the Traer Agua canyon, which is part of the greater Stoddard Range. The eastern side of the ridge is made up of Porphyritic Latite mid-Jurassic intrusive igneous rock and Cretaceous intrusive granitic rock. Both of these varieties are slow-cooled magma which form large crystals that provide good traction. Because of ancient water flows through the area, the volcanic rock is very featured (jugs, crimps, huecos, pockets, etc.). The rock color is deep red, almost appearing black at times due to the unusual type of volcanic activity. It is an amazing, metamorphic playground packed with great features!

Flora and Fauna

Water is scarce in the Lucerne Valley. The Creosote bushes, Joshua trees, Yucca, and scrub oak dot the barren landscape. You may encounter bobcats, coyotes, jack rabbits, or even a tortoise, if you're lucky. Watch out for snakes. Western Diamondback, and Pacific Diamondbacks are around but mostly found in Big Bear. Unfortunately, the venomous snake you're most likely to run into is the Mojave Green Rattlesnake. They are found in the 2,000-4,000 foot elevation zone and can be more than 10 times as poisonous as a Western Diamondback. These snakes have a blue-green color and diamonds on their backs that disappear as they approach the tail. If you get bitten by a snake, first call 911, and, if possible, have someone take a picture of the snake to show emergency personnel.

Weather

New Jack City is in the high desert. The average high temperature often exceeds 100 degrees in the summer with lows in the 60s. In the fall and winter, temperatures are in the 60s with lows dipping into the 30s and colder. Average rainfall is minimal with around 6" a year. As dry as it can be, when it does rain, thunderstorms and flash floods are common. Always check the local weather beforehand and, if you can, during your trip. The weather can change quickly, so be prepared.

Introduction

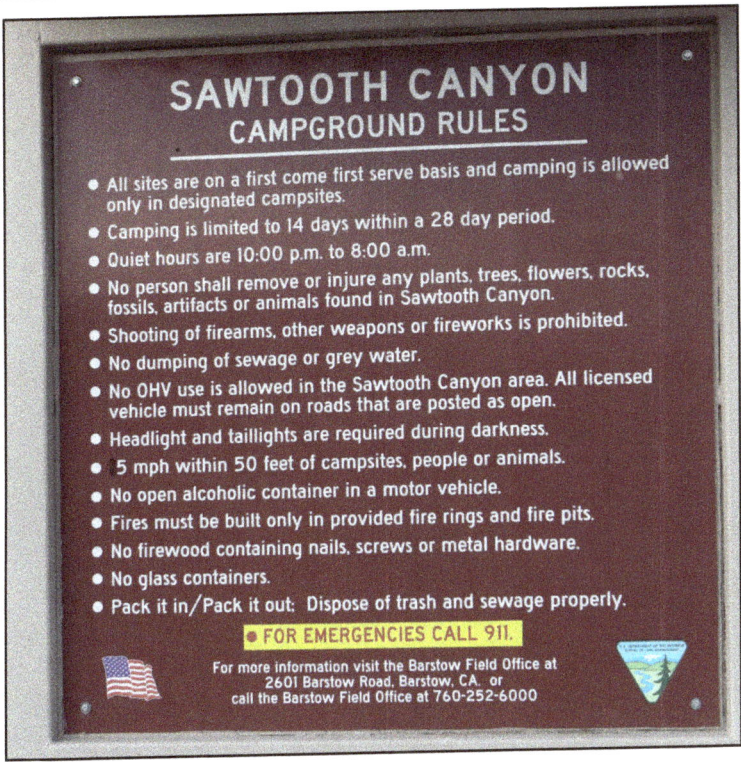

Camping

Sawtooth Canyon Campground IS New Jack City. There are 14 sites each with a concrete slab, table, gazebo, fire pit, and barbeque. The campground is open year round, and it's free (BLM Land, maximum 14 day stay). There are two vault toilets one by White Face crag and the other by the southern camp sites north of Boy Scout Wall (be sure to bring toilet paper). There is no water, and there are no trash receptacles in the canyon. You need to bring in everything you might need and take all that's left with you. There is a campground host near the entrance to the campground. Since the development of the campground, OHV access and shooting is no longer allowed within a half mile of the canyon. As of Fall 2015, there is no campground host, possibly due to funding issues. For more camping information, visit OnsightMedia.org

NO WATER AND NO TRASH at the campground. Plan accordingly.

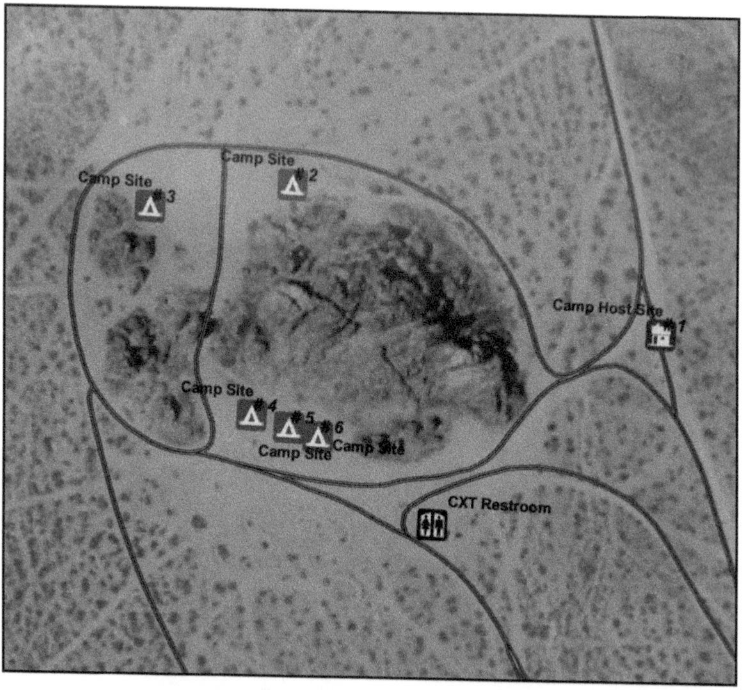
Camp Site
#3
Camp Site
#2
Camp Host Site
#1
Camp Site
#4
#5
#6
Camp Site
Camp Site
CXT Restroom

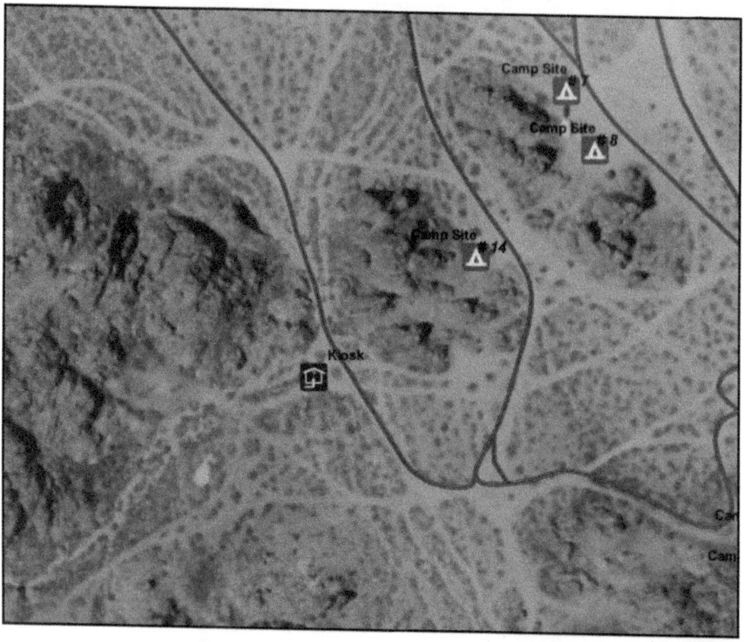
Camp Site
#7
Camp Site
#8
Camp Site
#14
Kiosk

Introduction

Etiquette

This is a popular campground for climbers and non-climbers alike. Please be respectful with music, leave no trace, etc. Show respect to the campground host, as they are only there to make sure things stay in order. Don't walk through occupied campgrounds to get to crags. Be polite and ask first or walk around. Basic campground etiquette will go a long way in maintaining harmony among everyone trying to enjoy the area. Use the provided vault toilets and **BRING TOILET PAPER**. Pack all of your trash out and leave no trace. Please be respectful of the effort and hard work that was put in to making this is a beautiful place where people come to enjoy the outdoors, the climbing, and the camping here.

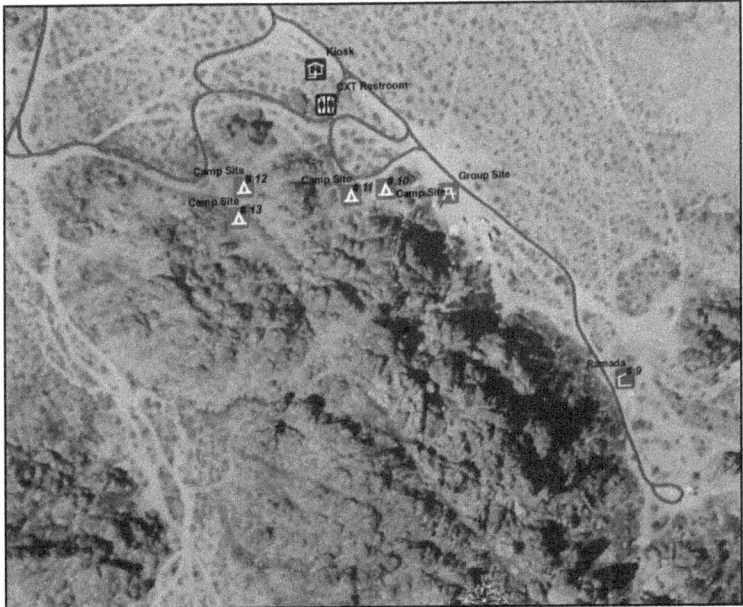

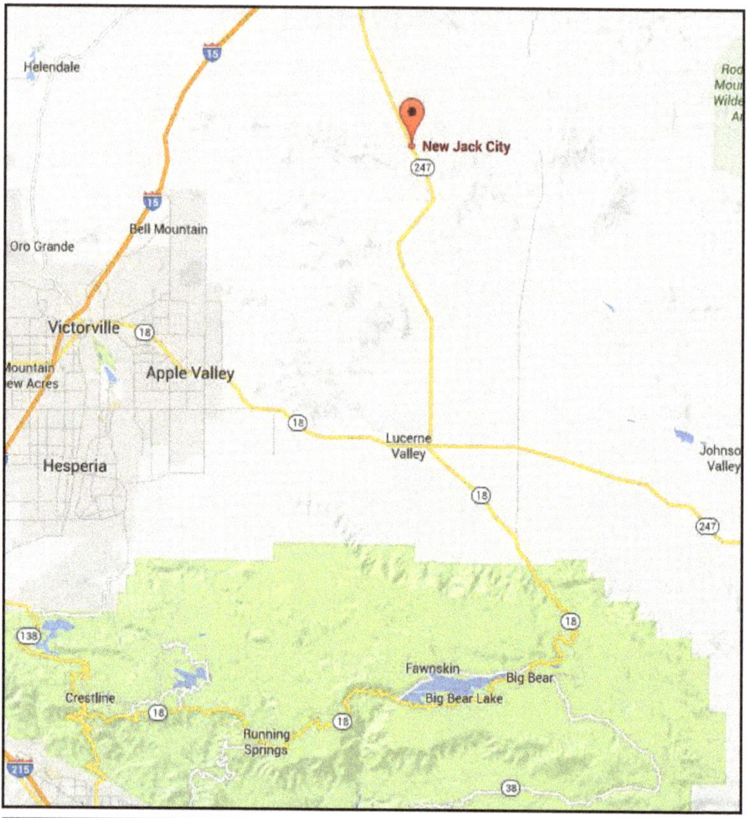

Helendale
15
New Jack City
247
15
Bell Mountain
Oro Grande
Victorville
18
Apple Valley
Hesperia
18
Lucerne Valley
18
247
18
138
Crestline
18
Running Springs
18
Fawnskin
Big Bear
Big Bear Lake
38
215

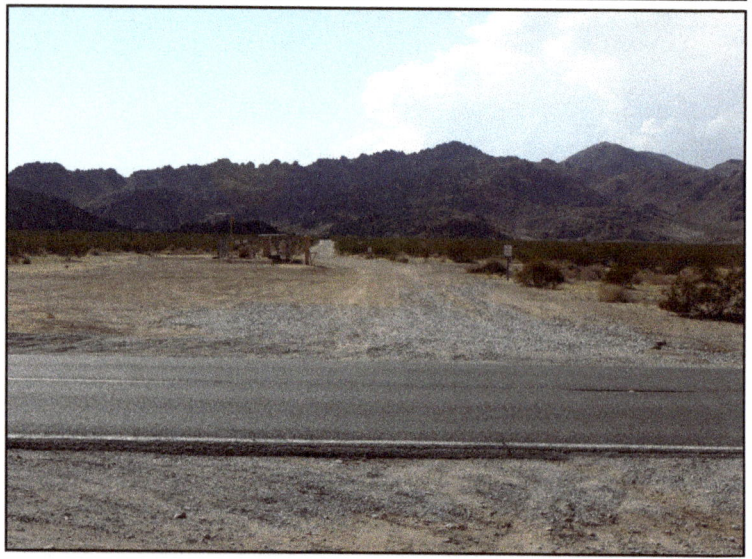

Introduction

Directions

From Las Vegas and Arizona, take either the 15 south or 40 west to Barstow. From the Inland Empire or LA Basin, take the 15 north to Barstow. From either direction, exit, and go south at the 247 (Barstow Road, Exit 183). Continue south on the 247 for about 15 miles. You will turn right on a dirt road that intersects the highway (34.681055, -116.966109)(See image below left). Continue westbound on the dirt road past the Sawtooth Canyon Campground sign.

From Big Bear (Holcomb Valley Pinnacles), it is a 45-minute drive. Take the 18 North (the "back way") out and down the mountain. At the first stop sign (a good 15-20 minutes), make a right onto Barstow Road (247 north). Continue 18 miles until you go over a mountain ridge, then make a left at the dirt road that intersects the highway (34.681055, -116.966109)(See image below left).

If you search "New Jack City, Lucerne Valley, CA" in Google Maps, you can get driving directions.

Estimated drive times:

20 Minutes	from Barstow
45 Minutes	from Holcomb Valley Pinnacles (Big Bear)
45 Minutes	from Victorville
1.5 hours	to Joshua Tree NP (S on 247, E on 62, follow signs)
1.5 hours	to the Inland Empire
1.5 hours	to Ontario Airport
1.5 hours	to Riverside Quarry
2 hours	to Orange County
2.5 hours	to Tahquitz and Suicide Rock
2.5 hours	to Las Vegas
2.5 hours	to Red Rock Canyon
2.5 hours	to LAX Airport
2.5+ hours	to Los Angeles
2.5 hours	to Oceanside
3 hours	to San Diego
3.5 hours	to Bishop
6 hours	to Yosemite Valley

All times are with no traffic! If you drive the 15 North on a Friday or South on a Sunday, you will fight heavy Las Vegas traffic (early mornings on those days aren't so bad). Plan accordingly to maximize time.

Local Resources

Bear Climbing - (909) 547-5449 (10am to 6pm everyday)(45-min Drive)
They stock the basics to keep you going.
39130 North Shore Drive, Fawnskin, CA 92333

REI in Rancho Cucamonga - (909) 646-8360 (1 hour away)
12218 E Foothill Blvd, Rancho Cucamonga, CA 91739
Hangar 18 in Rancho Cucamonga - (909) 476-1438 (1 hour away)
9004 Hyssop Dr, Rancho Cucamonga, CA 91730

Closest Hospital:
Barstow Community Hospital (ER) (20-minute drive)
820 E. Mountain View Street, Barstow, CA 92311
(760) 256-1761

Law Enforcement:
San Bernardino County Sheriff
32818 Verdugo Dr, Lucerne Valley, CA 92356
(760) 248-7655

Closest Food and Water (No water at NJC!):
Slash X Cafe: 6 miles north of New Jack City turn off.
Barstow is the next closest city at 15 miles away.

Count on having no mobile phone service in the canyon. To make any calls, emergency or not, you'll need to get back to the 247 to pick up coverage.

Introduction

Topo Legend

Black stars = Anchor locations
White stars = Bolt locations
Dashed white line = Bolt/route line

The placement of the stars are exactly over the bolt/anchor locations. Using high-resolution photos, stars were only placed when the bolt/anchor equipment could be seen. Always confirm in person, but use this as a starting point for preparation. Bolt locations can seem close together or spread out based on the angle of the photos. A majority of the bolts in New Jack City are painted, thus harder to spot.

Necessary Equipment

- 12-18 quickdraws

If you are bringing one rope, bring a 70m. Most routes can be done with a 60m, but there are quite a few that could be handled with 35m and 50m ropes.
Helmets are a good idea since there can be loose rock.

Crag Overview

Crag Overview

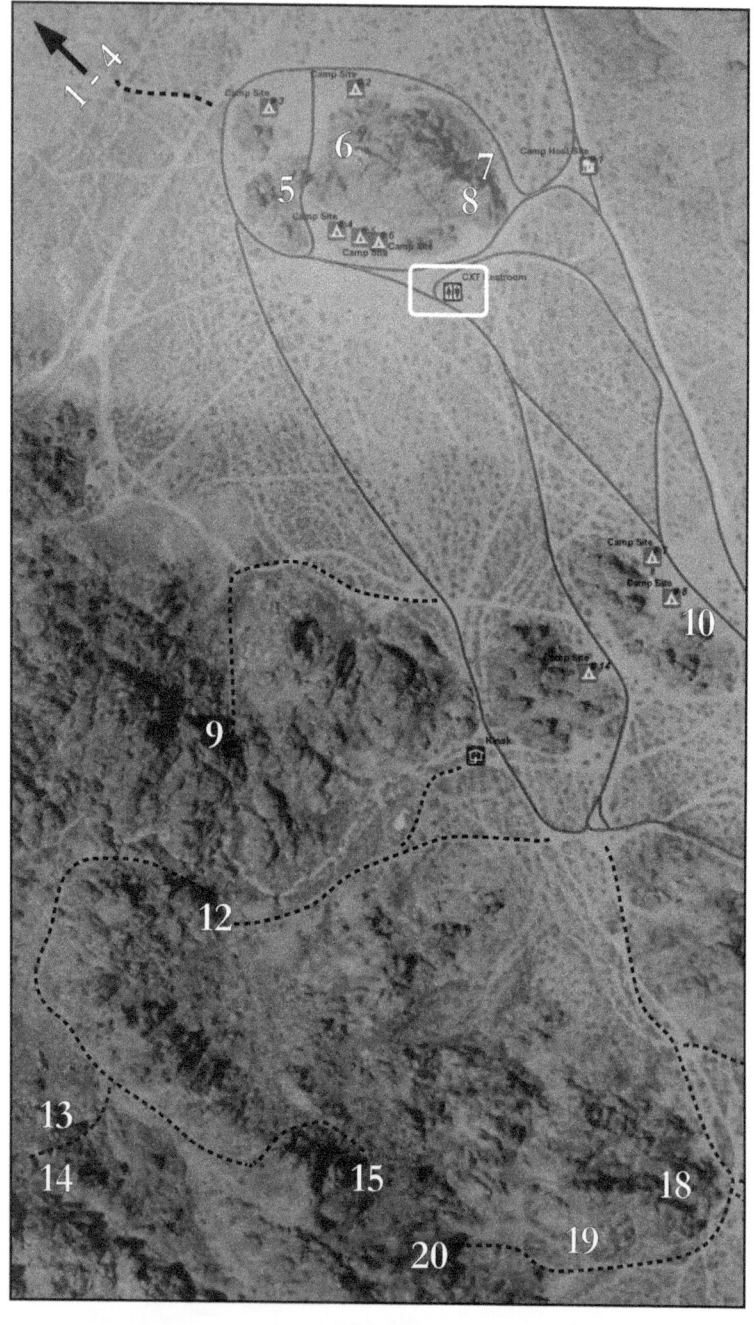

Crag Overview

Crag Overview

Entrance Area Crags

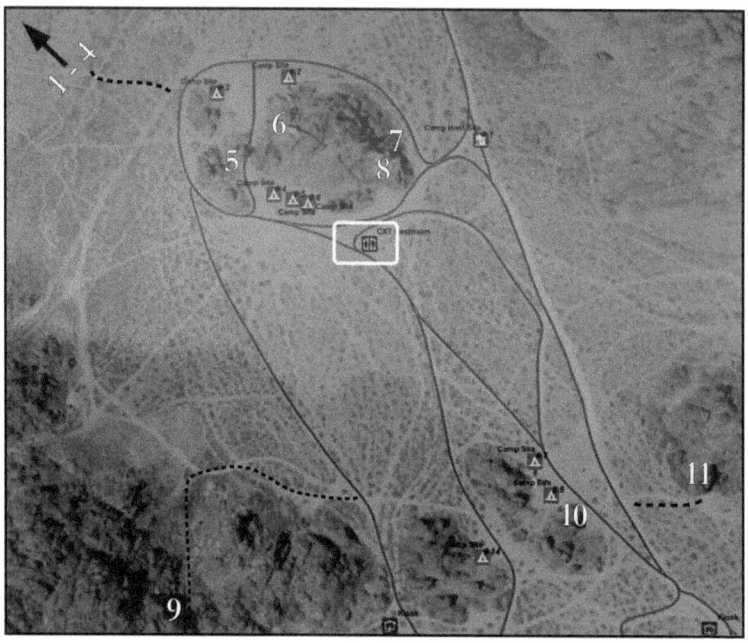

1. The Cave	Page	29
2. Leaning Tower	Page	33
3. Deadbolt Wall	Page	37
4. The Critic	Page	41
5. Intersection Rocks	Page	43
6. Valentine Wall	Page	47
7. The Snack Shop	Page	50
8. White Face	Page	52
9. White Streak Face	Page	57
10. Roadside West	Page	59
11. Roadside Crag	Page	61

The Land That Time Forgot

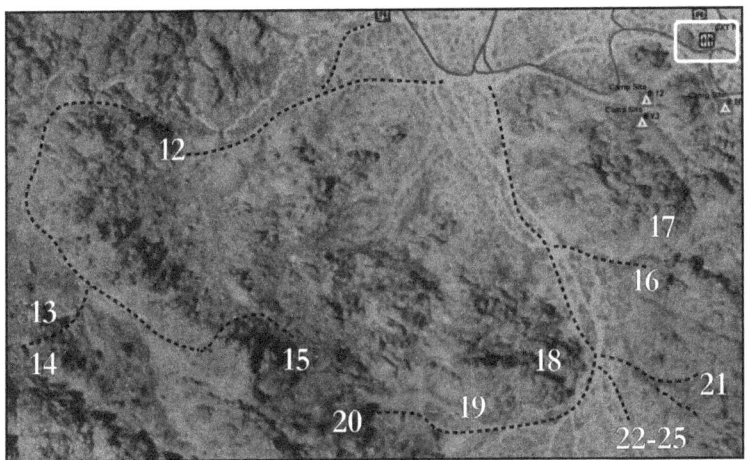

12. Bedrock Wall   Page   75
13. Bighorn Buttress   Page   77
14. Hidden Valley   Page   83
15. Dike Wall   Page   99

West Canyon Crags

16. Arch Rock   Page   107
17. Club Blute   Page   110
18. Sunshine Face   Page   115
19. Liz Hurley Boulder   Page   116
20. Predator Wall   Page   119
21. Dude Ranch   Page   135
22. Toy Block   Page   142
23. Korean Wall   Page   145
24. Cliffs of Insanity   Page   146
25. The Watchtower   Page   156

East Canyon Crags

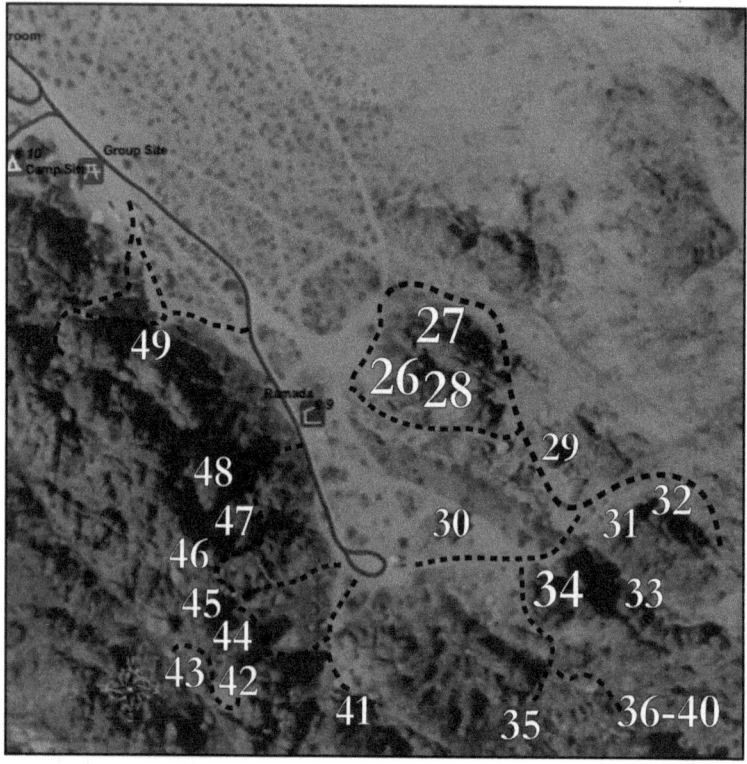

26. Parking Lot Rock	Page	175
27. Hidden Wall	Page	177
28. Sunnyside Crag	Page	179
29. Hueco Wall	Page	183
30. The Pinnacle	Page	189
31. Crucified Crag	Page	193
32. Beyond the Crucified	Page	197
33. Indirect Crag	Page	199
34. Raven Rocks	Page	201
35. The Getaway	Page	229
36. Raven's Roost	Page	236
37. The Shreen	Page	237

Crag Overview

East Canyon Crags

38. Nose Wall	Page	238
39. Fantasy Island	Page	239
40. The Fairway	Page	243
41. Hard Rock Cafe/Slab City	Page	249
42. The Finger	Page	253
43. Prodigy Pile	Page	255
44. Twin Towers	Page	257
45. Pat & Jack Pinnacle	Page	263
46. Lethal Rock	Page	267
47. The Fin	Page	271
48. Crossfire Crag	Page	273
49. Boy Scout Wall	Page	281

Entrance Area Crags

Entrance Area Crags

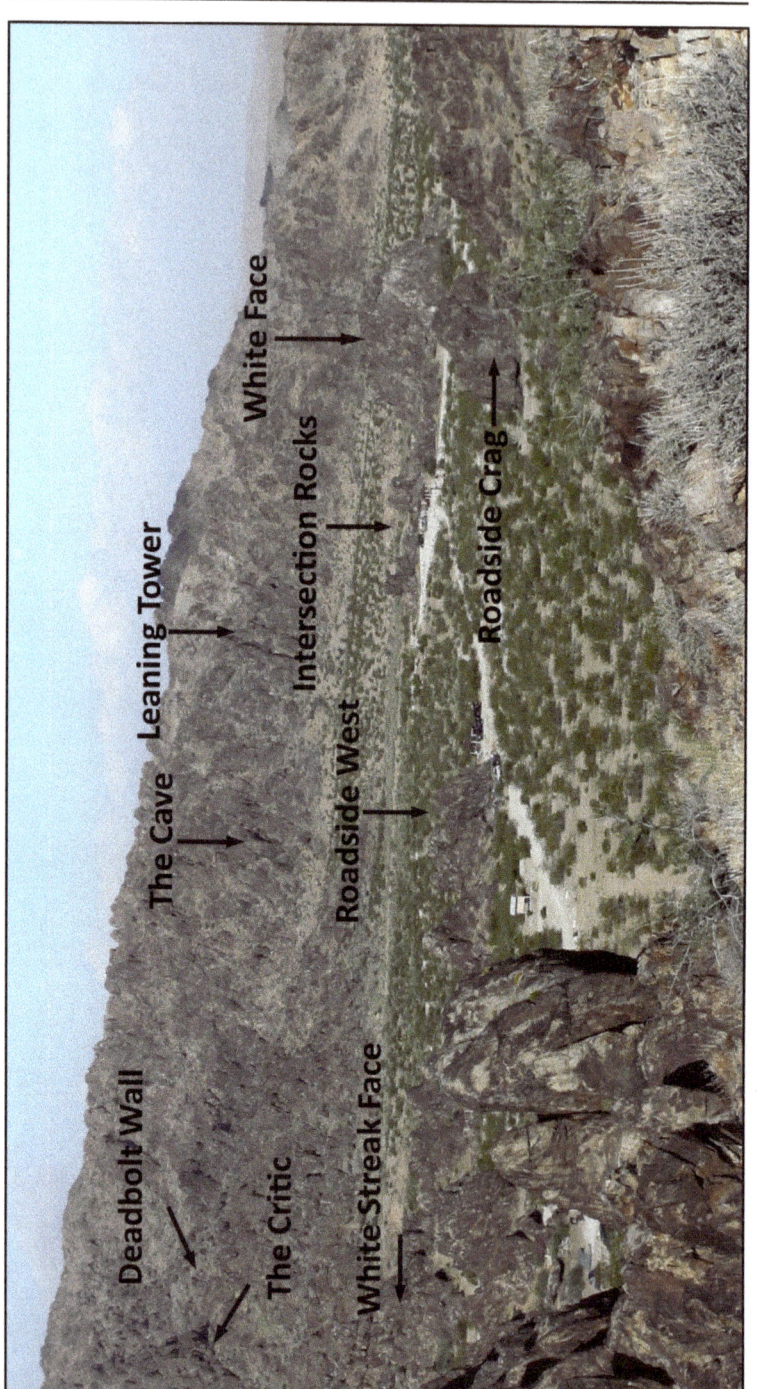

Entrance Area Crags

Since the development of Sawtooth Canyon Campground, the old road system has changed. The original road went toward and over the ridge (gas pipeline), but now you will be diverted left to the entrance. There you will see a kiosk with a map overview of the area and campground rules. From here, the road takes you south toward the campground host and the entrance area crags. The first thing you'll see as you drive in is the Snack Shop boulder problems on the backside of White Streak Face. The first five camp sites are situated around White Streak Face and Intersection Rocks. There is also a vault restroom (handicap accessible) and a dinosaur bone-themed playground.

The Cave and Leaning Tower are located on the hillside north of the campsites. It is about a 15-minute hike to get there from Camp 3 (best place to park). Deadbolt Wall and The Critic are on the mountaintop across the valley from and southwest of The Cave (hilltop on the north side of the pipeline road).

Farther south along the road are the Roadside crags. Once you pass that, you are entering the East Canyon.

Entrance Area Crags

Entrance Area Crags

The Cave

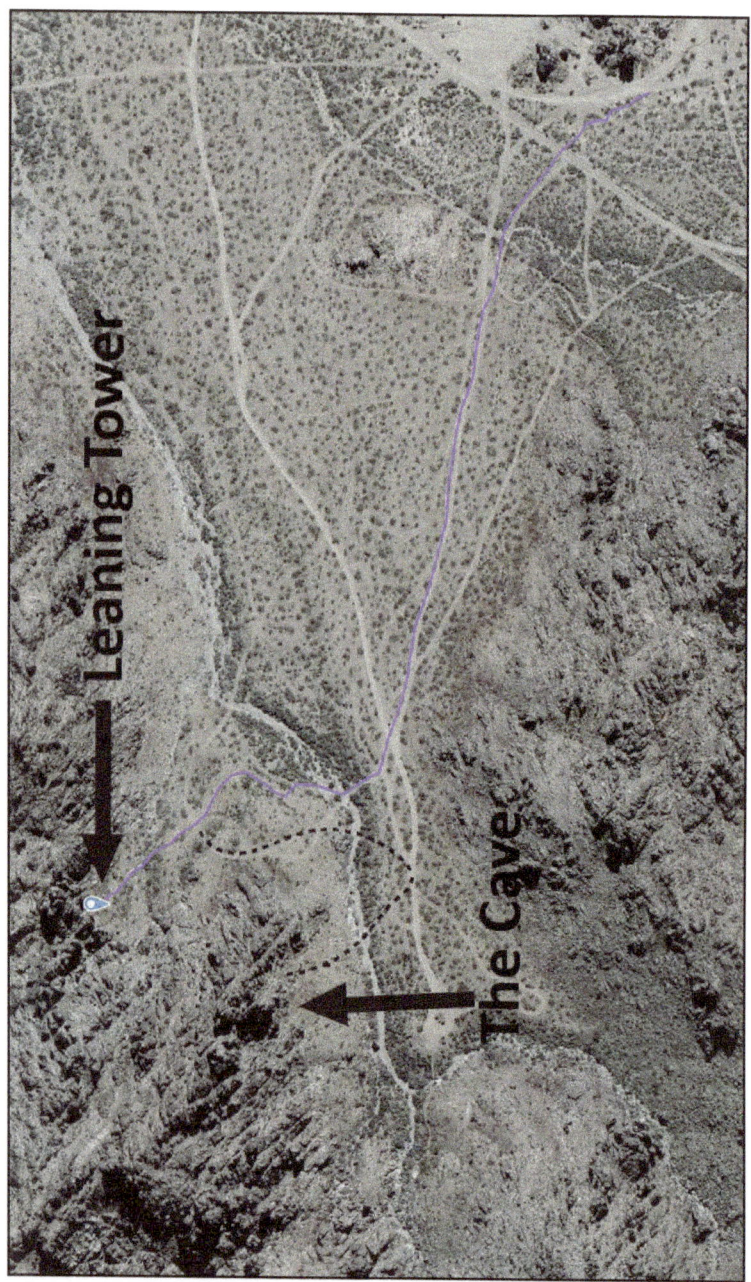

Entrance Area Crags

The Cave

Overview
The Cave lies on the ridge northeast of Camp 3. The climbing here is steep and difficult. There was an old road system that had a parking lot about 100 yards from the Cave, but it has been blocked off for years. The road is barely recognizable after being washed-out and reclaimed by the desert. Since it is not as easily accessible as before, it sees less traffic now than when you could park out front. This crag is in the sun year round.

Approach
Park at or around Camp 3. It's about a 10-minute hike along barely recognizable, washed-out roads. The trail gets harder to see the closer you get. Once you get a good view of the Cave, just keep aiming yourself toward it, and you'll get there. The satellite imagery is out of date, and nature has claimed this patch of desert again. There is a faint fork in the road where you can go left to the Cave or right to the Leaning Tower.

GPS: 34.672403, -116.990163

The Cave - West Face

1. Shell Shock 5.13b/c (50')
2. Sniper 5.12a/b (50')
3. On the Fringe 5.11d (50')
4. Cave Dweller 5.12b (50')
5. Project

Entrance Area Crags

The Cave

1. Shell Shock 5.13b/c (50')
Steep overhanging face climb.
Protection: 6 bolts, shut anchors

2. Sniper 5.12a/b (50')
Just right of Shell Shock. Slightly more solid holds and feet.
Protection: 5 bolts, shut anchors

3. On the Fringe ** 5.11d (50')
Up in the "cave." Starts at the base and climbs the fringe of the cave.
Protection: 6 bolts, shared chain anchors

4. Cave Dweller * 5.12b (50')**
A steep climb up the overhanging part of the cave.
Protection: 6 bolts, shared chain anchors

5. Project
Protection: 4 bolts, carabiner anchors

Entrance Area Crags

The Leaning Tower

Entrance Area Crags

The Leaning Tower

Overview
The Leaning Tower is on the same ridge and to the east of The Cave. Routes are on both the west and east face of the tall leaning spire. The rock is flaky, dark, and a menacing sight as you approach. There is one route on the west side that you have to scramble up a gully to get to the start. The other two are on the east side on a flat sloping gully with good belay spots. There is a decent amount of sun on this crag all year. Like the Cave, it's a bit of a hike compared to the average NJC approach.

Approach
Same approach as The Cave, but follow the solid line on the map below to arrive in front of the Leaning Tower. You'll stay right at the fork, and the last part of approach sees the trail disappear. Just Follow the route of least resistance and stay pointed toward the tower. It's easy to spot as you get closer.

GPS: 34.673181, -116.989728

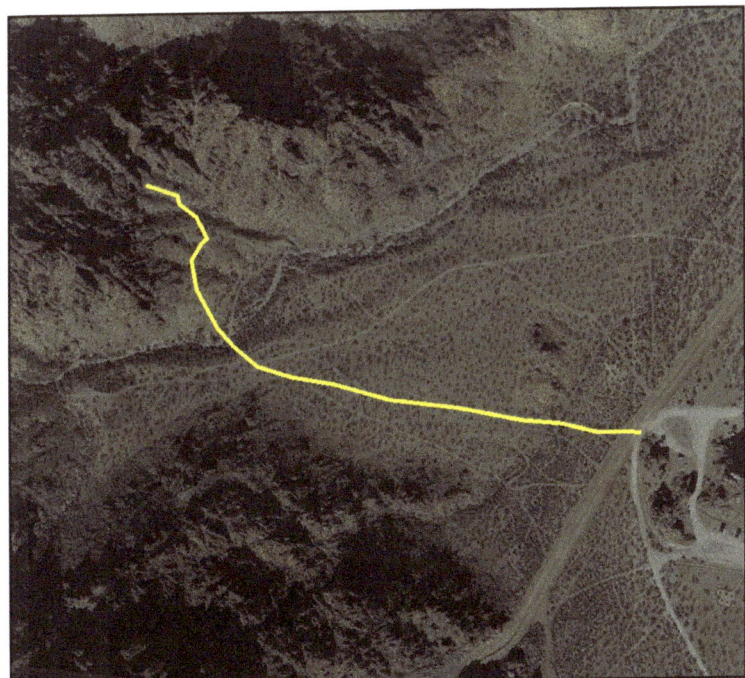

The Leaning Tower West Face

1. California Dreamin * 5.11a (70')
Scramble up the gully on the left of the Leaning Tower to reach the belay ledge and start.
Protection: 7 bolts, chain anchor

Entrance Area Crags

The Leaning Tower East Face

1. Life of the Party ** 5.11c (60')
Technical and tricky climb on the spire in front of the Leaning Tower. The start is just inside the right-side gully.
Protection: 6 bolts, chain anchor

2. Master of None ** 5.13b (90')**
Steep and long. Lots of features as you move past the middle and a little run out at the top.
Protection: 8 bolts, chain anchors

Deadbolt Wall

Entrance Area Crags

Deadbolt Wall

Overview
The Deadbolt Wall is on the south ridge across the valley (southwest) from The Cave. There are 5 routes on the Deadbolt Wall. The left four routes were developed by Louie Anderson. The far right route was developed by Tommy Thompson. Most of the routes start along a spine that runs up the gully. There is a little scrambling involved to start most of the routes. The belay areas can be a little precarious.

Approach
Similar approach to The Cave, but you will veer to the left (south) side of the valley and head up the to the ridge. Deadbolt Wall is the large, black-looking dome on the top right of the ridge as you approach.

GPS: 34.669816, -116.990146

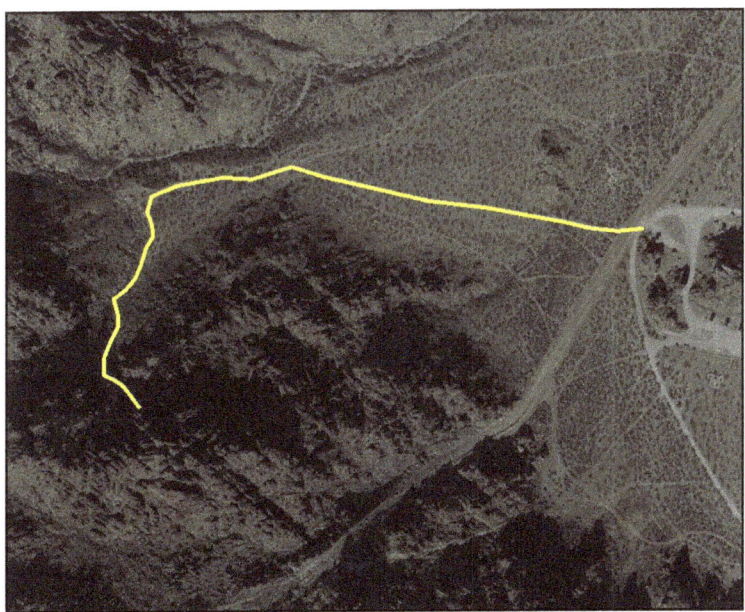

Deadbolt Wall

Entrance Area Crags

Deadbolt Wall

1. Headhunter 5.11b (40')
Protection: 4 bolts, shut anchors

2. The Meat 5.12c (50')
At the second bolt, traverse right through the third bolt of Tikiman and join Deadbolt at the 5th bolt.
Protection: 6 bolts, shut anchors

3. Tikiman 5.12b (50')
Protection: 6 bolts, shut anchors

4. Deadbolt 5.12c (60')
Protection: 6 bolts, shut anchors

5. Tommy Thompson Route 5.12a (50')
Protection: 7 bolts, chain anchors

The Critic

Entrance Area Crags 41

The Critic

Overview
The Critic is a single route that is on the south ridge across the valley from The Cave. This crag overlooks the entire New Jack City valley. The longer approach is rewarded with a very featured and challenging route.

Approach
Same approach as the Deadbolt Wall. Once you are on the ridge, continue left (south) around the spines that parallel the Deadbolt Wall. Follow the small "plateau" that wraps the ridge-line. The Critic will be on your right, facing east.

GPS: 34.669681, -116.988974

1. The Critic 5.12b (70')
Protection: 5 bolts, chain anchors

Intersection Rocks

Entrance Area Crags

Intersection Rocks

Overview
Intersection Rocks are short and to the point. Both crags are fully featured and serve as a quick option if you are staying in the northern camp site group. Both crags are south-facing with sun all day long. Developed by Louie Anderson.

Approach
Same driving approach as White Face, but continue on past it and the three camp sites. You can make a right onto the dirt through-road to get to the east crag or continue straight and around a curve to the right to the west crag. The east crag is literally on the dirt through-road (seen at the bottom of the image to the left). The west crag is about 50-75 feet to the west and on the same dirt road loop. They are both directly south of and kind of in Camp Site 3. Parking is plentiful, and there is a vault toilet nearby.

East Crag GPS: 34.670728, -116.984489
West Crag GPS: 34.670597, -116.984737

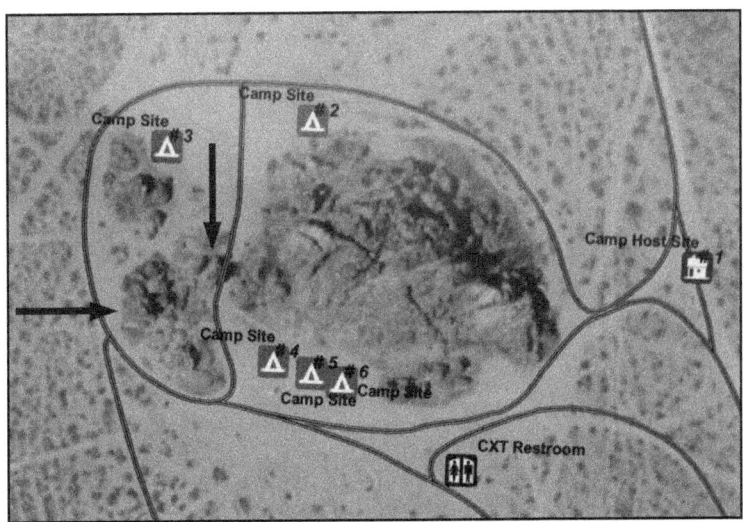

Tailgate Face

1. Crowd Pleaser 5.11b/c (30')
Start under the mini roof with a with side-pulls and a jug. Holds get smaller toward the top.
Protection: 3 bolts, chain anchors

2. Bumper Brigade 5.11a/b (30')
Start to the right of the mini roof to small huecos after the first bolt.
Protection: 3 bolts, chain anchors

3. Project 5.11a/b (30')(TR)
Protection: top rope

Entrance Area Crags

Intersection Rocks - West

1. Ape Index 5.11b (35')
Boulder-like start to big huecos and smaller pockets. Eventual lie-backs to good feet as you reach the top.
Protection: 4 bolts, chain anchors

Valentine Wall

Entrance Area Crags

Valentine Wall

Overview

Valentine Wall, one of the newest additions to New Jack City, is directly across the dirt through-road on the east side of Camp Site 3. There are some fun, moderate routes in the shade most of the day.

Approach

Same approach as White Face, but continue on past it and the three camp sites. You will make a right onto the dirt through-road, and the wall will be on your right facing camp site 3. It's about a 2-minute walk from most parking in the area.

GPS: 34.670935, -116.984143

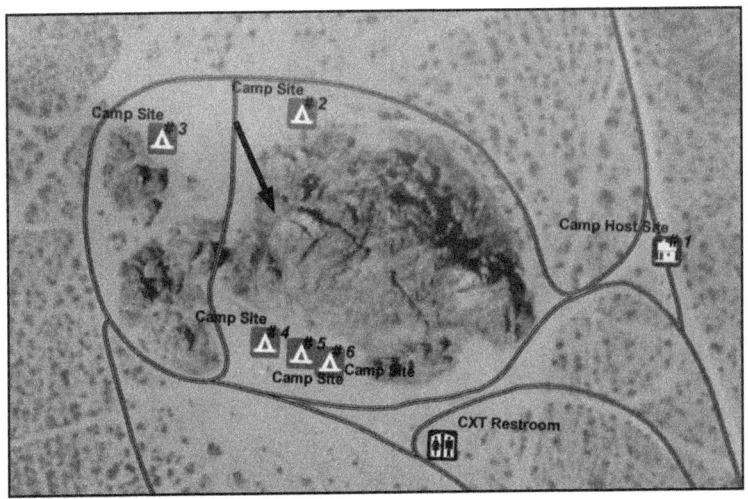

Valentine Wall

Entrance Area Crags

Valentine Wall

1. My Bloody Valentine * 5.10a (70')**
Around the back side of the wall. Vertical and fun route with balancy moves. Climb the weakness and clip out left all the way up..
Protection: 6 bolts, screw-link anchors

2. Victoria's Secret * 5.8 (70')**
Smaller holds at the start but larger flakes and jugs as you go up. The route will move left toward a large crux bulge before the anchors.
Protection: 6 bolts, ring anchors

3. Cupid's Fever * 5.8 (80')**
Start below the jagged flake and up toward solid feet and a more featured face. A fun, long climb. Its a little run out and dirty after the last bolt when reaching the anchors.
Protection: 7 Bolts, ring anchors

Audrey Robbins on Cupid's Fever

The Snack Shop

Overview

The Snack Shop is on the north side of White Face crag and can be seen on the right side of the road as you enter the campground. There are two boulder problems that are great for warming up or killing time waiting for the rest of your party. The rock quality is pretty good, and there are usually clear chalk marks going up and through the gully.

Approach

As you approach the campground host, the road will veer to the right and come to a fork. Make a right at the fork, and in about 100' you'll be at the Snack Shop. There is enough room to park a couple cars right out front. If the small lot is full, park over by the restroom on the other side of the crag and walk around. It's a 2- minute walk from the other side (White Face Crag).

GPS: 34.670843, -116.983289

Entrance Area Crags 51

The Snack Shop

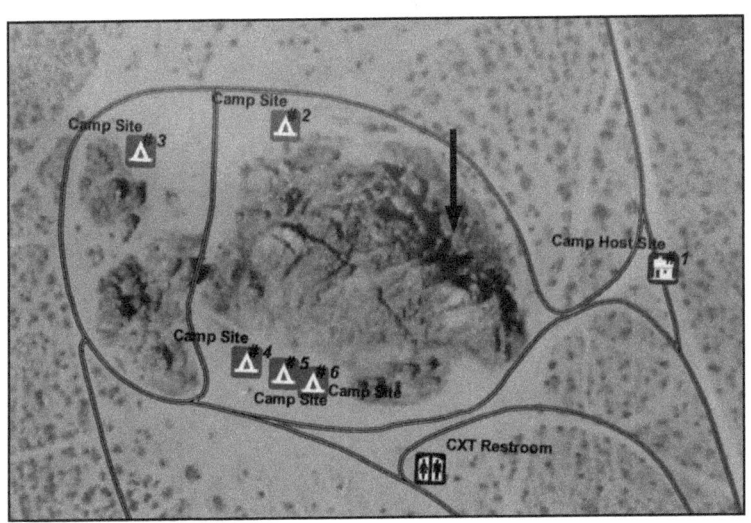

1. The Hall V-Easy (65')
This is the long traverse up and into the gully. The start is at the beginning of the line marker with some obvious jugs. This is a great spot to get warmed up or to do laps up and down. The ground rises with the gully to the top so stepping off if needed is pretty safe.

2. The Low IQ V-Easy (15')
This is located to the right and in front of the gully. Another quick warm-up spot, which goes up instead of The Hall traverse. You might feel a little more exposed on this one.

White Face

Overview

White Face is the southsfacing crag in the entrance formation. The height ranges from 35'-45' and grades from 5.6-5.11a. The routes here are more technical. There is something for everyone, and it is a nice place to set up shop if your party climbs at various grades. You can't camp directly in front, but there are three sites just left of the picture above. All-day sun can clear this place out in the summer and provide warm rock in the winter. There are some very high-quality routes here and, if in the main area, it would see a ton more traffic.

Approach

As you approach the campground host, the road will veer to the right and come to a fork. Make a left at the fork, and in about 100' you'll see the parking spots for White Face on your right. There is enough room to park three cars right out front with a ton of parking around this whole formation. Please be respectful of the camp site parking spots. If the sites are occupied, then the spots in front of them are reserved for the campers.

GPS: 34.670666, -116.983345

Entrance Area Crags

White Face

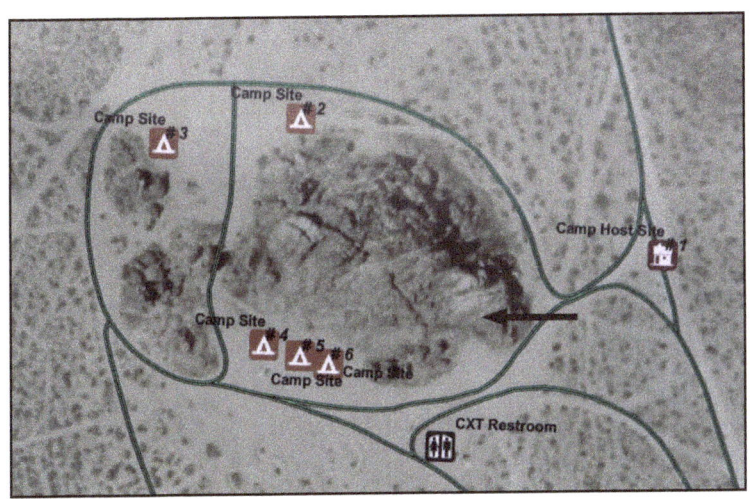

White Face

1. **White Head 5.9 (40')**
2. **Stemroids 5.11a (45')**
3. **White Out 5.10b (45')**
4. **Snow White 5.10d (45')**
5. **Whiter Shade of Pale 5.6 (35')**
6. **White Flight 5.7 (35')**

There used to be quite a bit of graffiti on this wall. It has since been cleaned up and is in great shape, but it can definitely be overlooked because of the sun exposure. The close proximity to the camp sites and the varying degrees of difficulty really make this a one-stop shop for a group with various skill levels.

Entrance Area Crags 55

White Face

1. White Head ** 5.9 (40')
The farthest left route on the wall, "White Head" is a good warm-up with a boulder-like start up a steep face. A fair amount of jugs with some edges thrown in make it a challenging yet fun route.
Protection: 4 bolts, shut anchors

2. Stemroids ** 5.11a (45')
A few lie-back moves to gain the first bolt, then it eases up a bit in the middle. Once you hit the upper section, there are more lie-backs until an awkward crux at the top. Definitely the hardest on the wall, but more ok due to the awkward movements.
Protection: 5 bolts, shut anchors

3. White Out *** 5.10b (45')
A little easier than Stemroids, this route has some technical moves with a jug here and there to rest. Some hard moves to gain the first bolt. An excellent route for the grade.
Protection: 5 bolts, shut anchors

4. Snow White *** 5.10d (45')
Bouldering-like start to a higher-than-normal first bolt. This is a slowly steepening climb all the way to the top. Lots of solid holds and features
Protection: 5 bolt, chain anchors

5. Whiter Shade of Pale ** 5.6 (35')
A little bit of everything on this route. A crack option, good hands, and solid moves. A great short beginner route that will be overlooked by most because of the location. Slick rock and a difficult start. In the shade year round.
Protection: 4 bolts, shared shut anchors with White Flight

6. White Flight * 5.7 (35')
Great beginning leader route. Lots of solid footholds and handholds to the top. A cleaner and more challenging route than its neighbor, Whiter Shade of Pale. Slick rock and a difficult start. In the shade year round.
Protection: 4 bolts, shared shut anchors with Whiter Shade of Pale

There is a high-ball boulder problem to the left of White Head. It starts in the soot stained notch.

Entrance Area Crags

White Streak Face

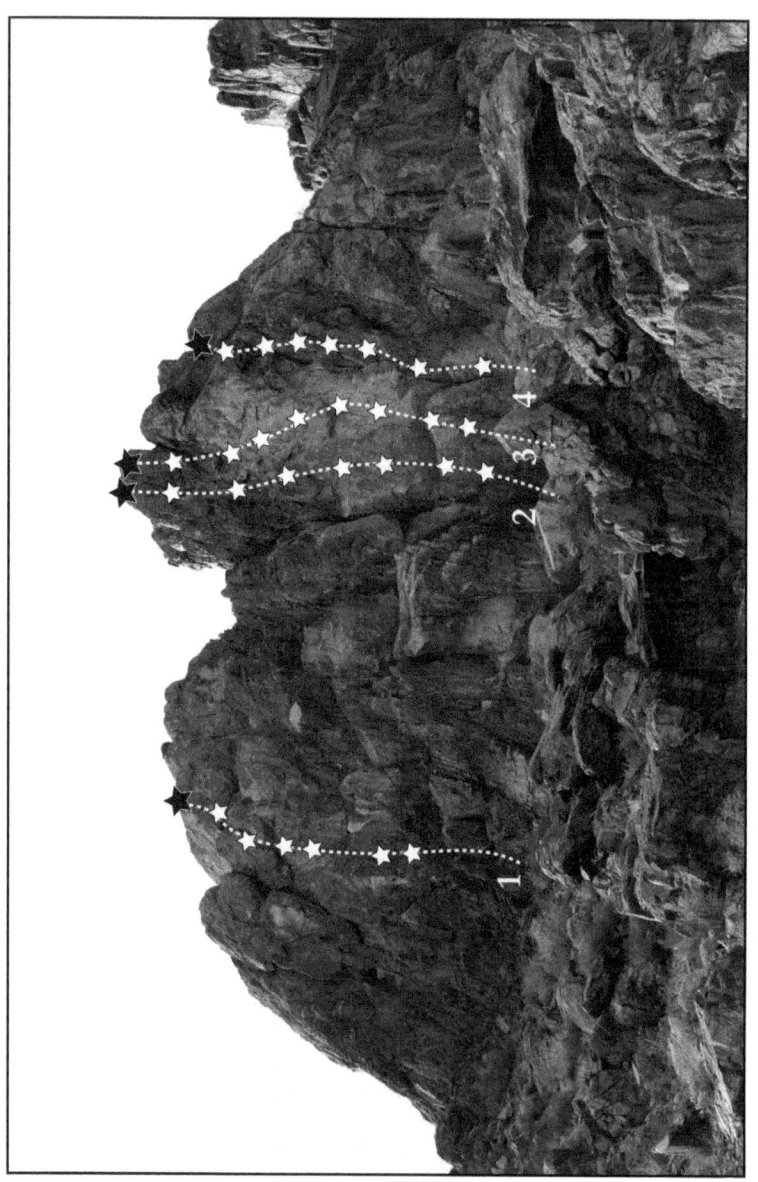

Entrance Area Crags

White Streak Face

Overview
White Streak Face is a north-facing crag with only a little bit of sun in the mornings. The roads no longer go directly in front, so traffic has died down compared to more easily accessible crags in the canyon. There are four challenging routes on the north face.

Approach
Take the far west road south from Camp Site 3 and White Face. There is no longer a turnoff, so park alongside the road and hike in a couple hundred feet. The trail is pretty obvious and will curve aroundto the southeast to reach the crag. Scramble up to the belay notch at the base of the wall.

GPS: 34.668229, -116.983868

0a. You Just Got Jacked 5.10a (65')(No topo, leftmost route)
Furthest left bolted route on the end arete.
Shares anchors with Oh Behive.
Protection: 3 bolts to 2 fixed draws to 1 bolt, shared chain anchors

0b. Oh Behive 5.11a (65')(No topo, right of You Just Got Jacked)
Just right of and shares anchors with You Just Got Jacked.
Protection: 6 bolts, shared chain anchors

1. Hang Daddy ** 5.11b (65')
Right of Oh Behive.
Protection: 6 bolts, chain anchors

2. Generous Portions ** 5.10b (80')
Left side of the White Streak.
Protection: 7 bolts, chain anchors

3. Use Your Mind * 5.11a (80')**
Route is on the white streak.
Protection: 8 bolts, chain anchors

4. Dry Spell ** 5.9 (65')
Furthest right route on the face.
Protection: 7 bolts, chain anchors

Roadside West

Entrance Area Crags

Roadside West

Overview
Directly next to Camp Site 8. A decent top rope route on the North side and a couple technical routes on the south face (pictured left).

Approach
You can park right next to the north face by Camp Site 8. See the overview map on the previous pages.

GPS: 34.668247, -116.981784

(Pictured above)
1. N00b Slab 5.6 (45') (Top Rope)
Scramble up the side (white line above) to reach the anchor bolts on top. Great for beginners.

(Pictured left)
2. Westward Ho * 5.11d (45') (South face) (3 bolts, chain anchors)
3. She Packs Her Bags for Outer Space * 5.11b (45') (south face) (same)

Entrance Area Crags

Roadside Crag

Entrance Area Crags

Roadside Crag

Overview

Roadside Crag used to be the most accessible crag, but since the development of the campground and reorganization of the roads, it is no longer on the roadside. Roadside has a handful of steep to really steep routes on the south side and a few easier routes on the north face. The main wall, which is south-facing, is in the sun in the morning and can provide shade in the afternoon. The north side is always in the shade.

Approach

Approach is the same for Roadside West. Use the Roadside West parking area and walk directly east to Roadside Crag. It is the obvious overhanging crag on its own.

GPS: 34.668456, -116.980560

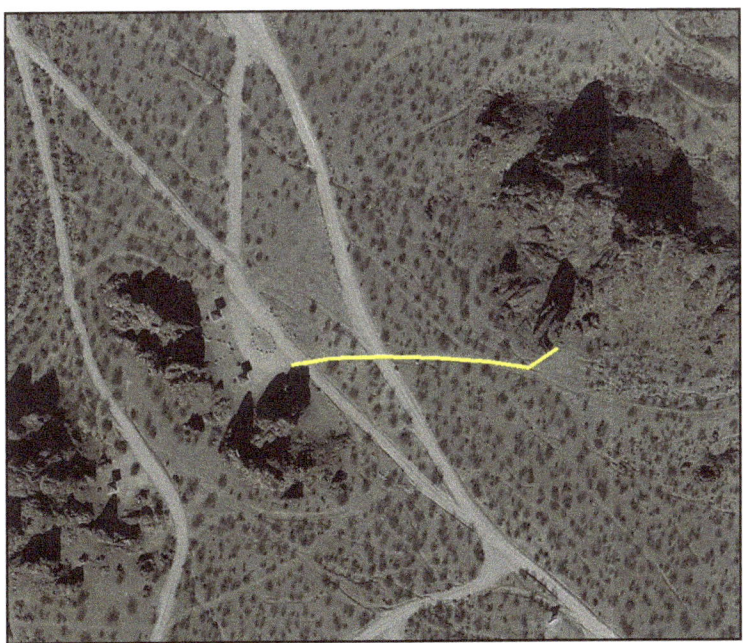

Roadside Crag - North

Entrance Area Crags

Roadside Crag

1. Roadside Warrior * 5.9 (50')**
Tricky face climb that eventually traverses over to shares anchors with My Side of the Roadside.
Protection: 6 bolts, shared chain anchors

2. My Side of the Roadside ** 5.7 (50')
Easy face climb with a lot of features. Shares anchors with Roadside Warrior.
Protection: 4 bolts, shared chain anchors

Roadside Crag - South

Entrance Area Crags

Roadside Crag - South

1. Clumsy* 5.12a (40')**
Very technical with little room for error. Shares anchors with Hateful Little Girl.
Protection: 4 bolts, shared shut anchors

2. Hateful Little Girl 5.12b (40')
Shares anchors with Clumsy and Madam X.
Protection: 4 bolts, shared shut anchors

3. Madam X 5.12c (50') (TR)
Easy face climb with a lot of features. Shares anchors with Clumsy and Hateful Little Girl.
Protection: Top rope, shared shut anchors

4. Propaganda * 5.11b (40')
Shares anchors with Roadside Warrior.
Protection: 5 bolts, shut anchors

5. You Get What You Deserve * 5.12d (50')**
Protection: 5 bolts, chain anchors

6. Lost in the Middle ** 5.12b (50')**
Straight up the steep face.
Protection: 5 bolts, chain anchors

7. Guilty as Sin ** 5.12b (50')
Starts up Lost in the Middle and breaks off right and joins Guilt Free for the finish. Shares anchors with Guilt Free.
Protection: 6 bolts, shared chain anchors

8. Guilt Free ** 5.12b (50')
The last bolted route on the right. Boulder-like start then straight up the steep face. Finish over the bulge and up to the anchors.
Protection: 5 bolts, shared chain anchors

The Land That Time Forgot

Area Overview

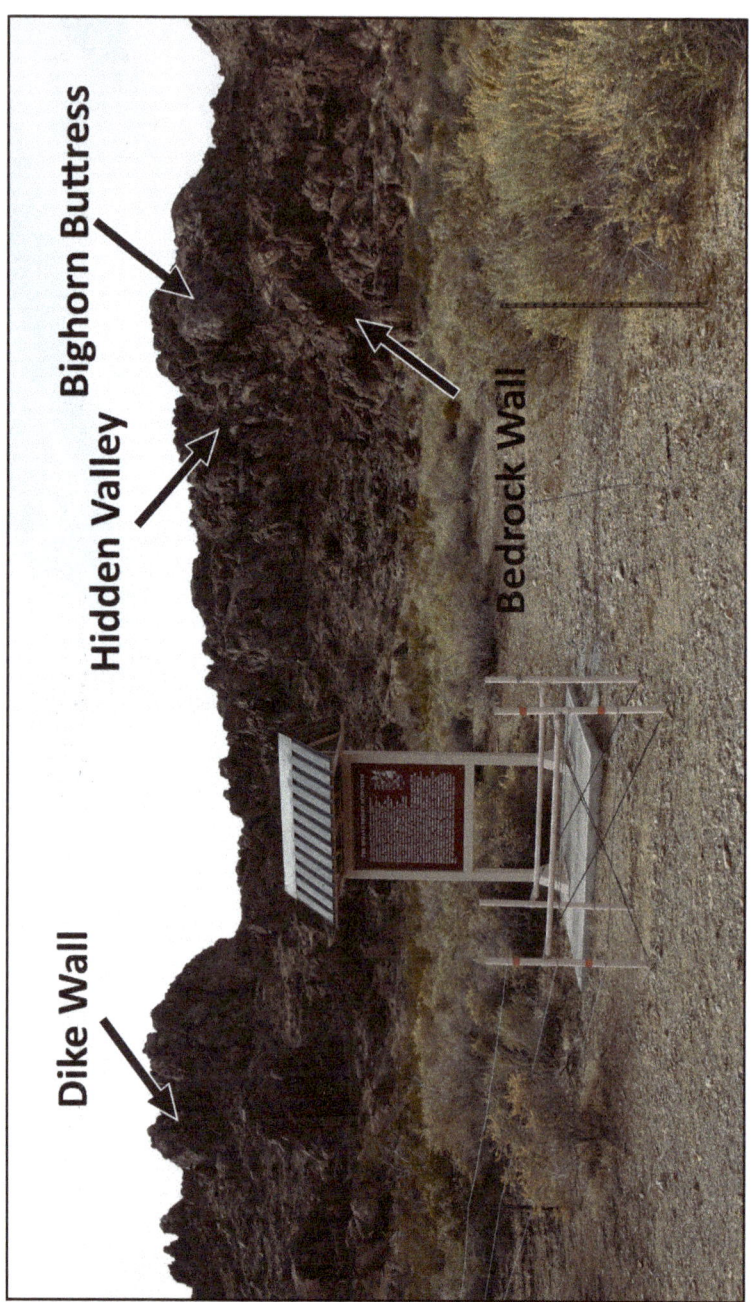

The Land That Time Forgot

Area Overview

Overview
The Land That Time Forgot is a new area with a lot of development. There are multiple new crags all within a 15-minute approach. The area is located on the big ridge just north of the West Canyon area. Most areas are east-facing. Some of the best quality routes in the area can be found here. Everything in this area was previously unpublished/undocumented and has seen little traffic over the last 10 years or so. Extensive cleaning was performed during the winter of 2015.

Approach
The parking area is north of the Predator Wall parking area. There is a small turn off with a kiosk just south of the White Streak Face trailhead. This is the main entrance to The Land That Time Forgot. There is additional parking by the West Canyon trail head (Predator Wall parking).

GPS: 34.667545, -116.983219

Area Overview

The Land That Time Forgot

Area Overview

The view from Hidden Valley area

The Land That Time Forgot

Bedrock Wall

The Land That Time Forgot

Bedrock Wall

Overview
Bedrock Wall is one of the newly developed crags in New Jack City. This wall is east-facing and is on the trail leading up to Big Horn Buttress valley.

Approach
Once you pass the main kiosk and the Campground Host, take the road to the left of White Face at the fork. Continue past the vault toilet and camp sites. Make a left at the "T" intersection and drive south. After passing White Streak Face on your right, you will see a trailhead kiosk. Park in front of the fence. Follow the beaten path. You can see the wall from the kiosk. (The white catch basin and watering hole is for the native Bighorn Sheep).

Parking lot GPS: 34.666676, -116.985129

1. Fred * 5.9 (65')**
Boulder-like crux at the first bolt then slab climbing to the steep finish.
Protection: 8 bolts, chain anchors

2. Barney ** 5.8 (65')
Start up the initial slab and cross over to the main face. Steep finish.
Protection: 8 bolts, chain anchors

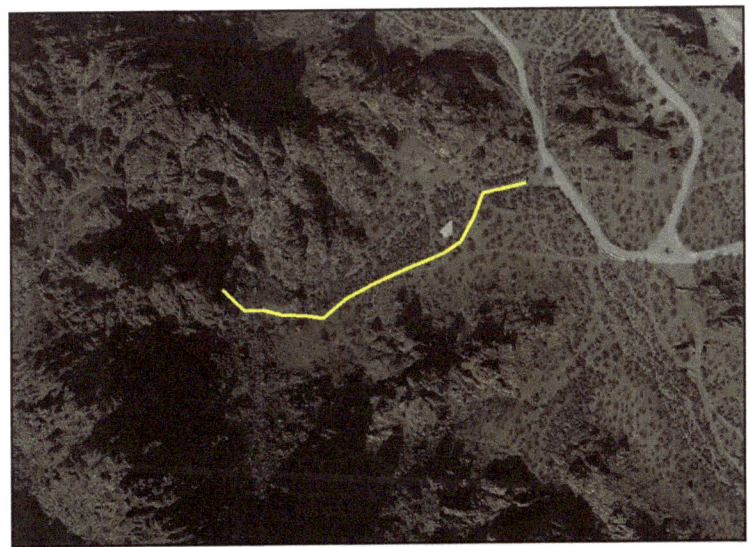

Bighorn Buttress

The Land That Time Forgot

Bighorn Buttress

Overview

Bighorn Buttress is one of the most recently developed crags in New Jack City. This large crag is up on the ridge west of the Predator Wall parking area. It is about a 15-minute approach along a steep trail ascending around 400 feet. There are some great routes here, including (according to Sam and Jack) the best 5.10 in New Jack City, "Catalina."

Approach

Same approach as Bedrock Wall but keep following the trail as it wanders northwest along the formation. Hug the formation on your left until it opens up on an upper valley. Follow the trail back south and watch for the fork that zigzags west up the mountain. There are multiple cairns marking the trail. Bighorn Buttress is hard to miss and stands out on the ridge. Try and find the main trail to minimize the impact on the area.

GPS: 34.665798, -116.987621

Bighorn Buttress

The Land That Time Forgot

Bighorn Buttress

1. Poaching Bighorns * 5.10b (60')**
Start in the belay notch at the base and in the middle of Bighorn Buttress. Climb the skinny weakness to the top.
Protection: 9 bolts, chain anchors

2. Catalina ** 5.10c (60')**
One of the best 5.10s that New Jack City has to offer. Start on the boulder and up the small cracks and around the bulge to the main face.
Protection: 7 bolts, chain anchors

Bighorn Buttress

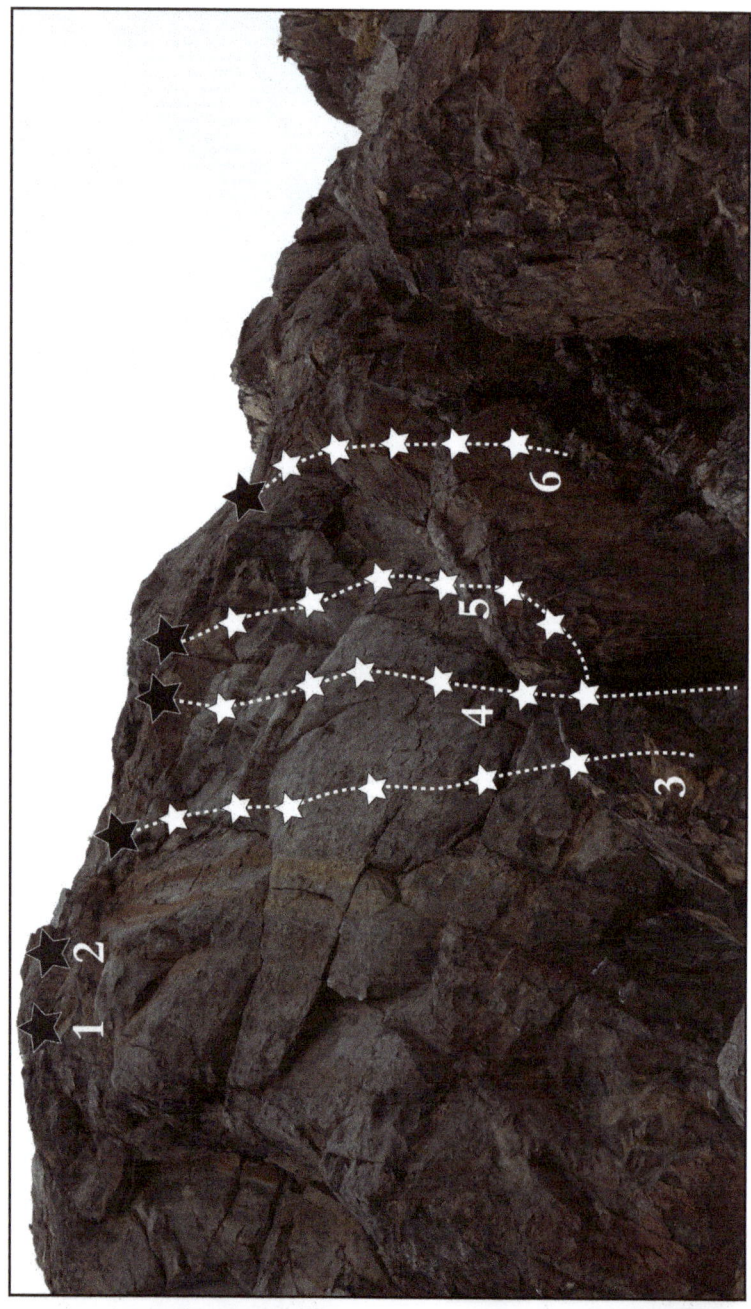

The Land That Time Forgot

Bighorn Buttress

3. All I Can Grab *** 5.10d (60')
Start in the gully to the right of Catalina. Face climb to the blocky section right of the orange markings.
Protection: 6 bolts, chain anchors

4. Legion of Evil *** 5.11a (60')
Just to the right of and a harder version of All I Can Grab.
Protection: 6 bolts, chain anchors

5. The Snake *** 5.10d (60')
Start with Legion of Evil and move right and up at the first bolt.
Protection: 7 bolts, chain anchors

6. Toxic Box ** 5.11a (30')
20 feet right of The Snake.
Protection: 5 bolts, chain anchors

Hidden Valley

The Land That Time Forgot

Hidden Valley

Overview
Hidden Valley is on the large ridge overlooking the entrance area crags and campsites. There are three walls in the upper valley and two walls in the lower tier. The rock quality here, as with most of the The Land That Time Forgot, is excellent. This area is brand new and full of quality routes. If the main valley is windy or hot, this is the place to be. It is completely protected from wind and has an amazing view. Lots of shade all year round. Even though it has the longest approach in all of NJC, you will definitely be rewarded here.

Approach
Same approach as Bighorn Buttress. The entrance to the Hidden Valley is just to the right of Drunken Midget Wrestling. It is a sketchy scramble to get up there, but it's worth it. You can also scramble up to the left of Bighorn Buttress to a small tunnel that can be crawled through to the Hidden Valley.

GPS: 34.665374, -116.987393

Hidden Valley - Lower Tier

The Land That Time Forgot

Hidden Valley - Lower Tier

These routes are located below the valley, left and around the corner from Drunken Midget Wrestling.

1. Gonna Be Just Like Them ** 5.10c (55')
Protection: 7 bolts, chain anchors

2. Chemical Warfare 5.11d (60')
Protection: 6 bolts, chain anchors

Drunken Midget Wrestling

The Land That Time Forgot

Drunken Midget Wrestling

Overview
One route about 100 feet to the left (south) of Big Horn Buttress. Right at the entrance of the Hidden Valley, Drunken Midget Wrestling is on the lower tier of the valley.

Approach
Same approach as Bighorn Buttress but about 100' south along the ridge. The entrance to the Hidden Valley is in the same spot.

Parking lot GPS: 34.665798, -116.987621

1. Drunken Midget Wrestling 5.11a (70')
A long right-traversing route with fixed draws to the top. You can top out in the Hidden Valley.
Protection: 17 fixed chain draws, chain draw anchors

Hidden Valley - South Wall

Hidden Valley - South Wall

1. Power Grab 5.12a/b (40')
Climb down to the start below and left into the gully from Hangman.
Protection: Bolts to chain anchors

2. Hangman 5.12a (40')
Protection: 4 bolts, chain anchors

3. Nervous Breakdown 5.12a (40')
Protection: 5 bolts, chain anchors

4. Gallows Pole 5.10c (40')
Protection: 5 bolts, chain anchors

Hidden Valley - South Wall

5. Violent Arrest 5.11+ (30')
Protection: 3 bolts, chain anchors

The Land That Time Forgot

Hidden Valley - West Wall

1. Tradliness 5.11c (55')
2. Waiting For Anarchy *** 5.11b (55')
3. Idiots at Happy Hour *** 5.10a (55')

Hidden Valley - West Wall

1. Tradliness 5.11c (55')
Follow the small dihedral up the wall through powerful and technical moves. Crux toward the top when moving on to the face.
Protection: 6 bolts, chain anchors

2. Waiting For Anarchy * 5.11b (55')**
Standout route with sustained difficulty on excellent rock.
Protection: 5 bolts, chain anchors

3. Idiots at Happy Hour * 5.10a (55')**
Hand jam start to first bolt. Slick rock to start. Stay left of the crack up the face. Crux is just below the huge jug horn.
Protection: 6 bolts, chain anchors

Hidden Valley - North Wall

Hidden Valley - North Wall

Jack Marshall at Hidden Valley (December 2015).

The Land That Time Forgot

Hidden Valley - North Wall

Sam Owings on the North Wall of Hidden Valley (December 2015).

Hidden Valley - North Wall

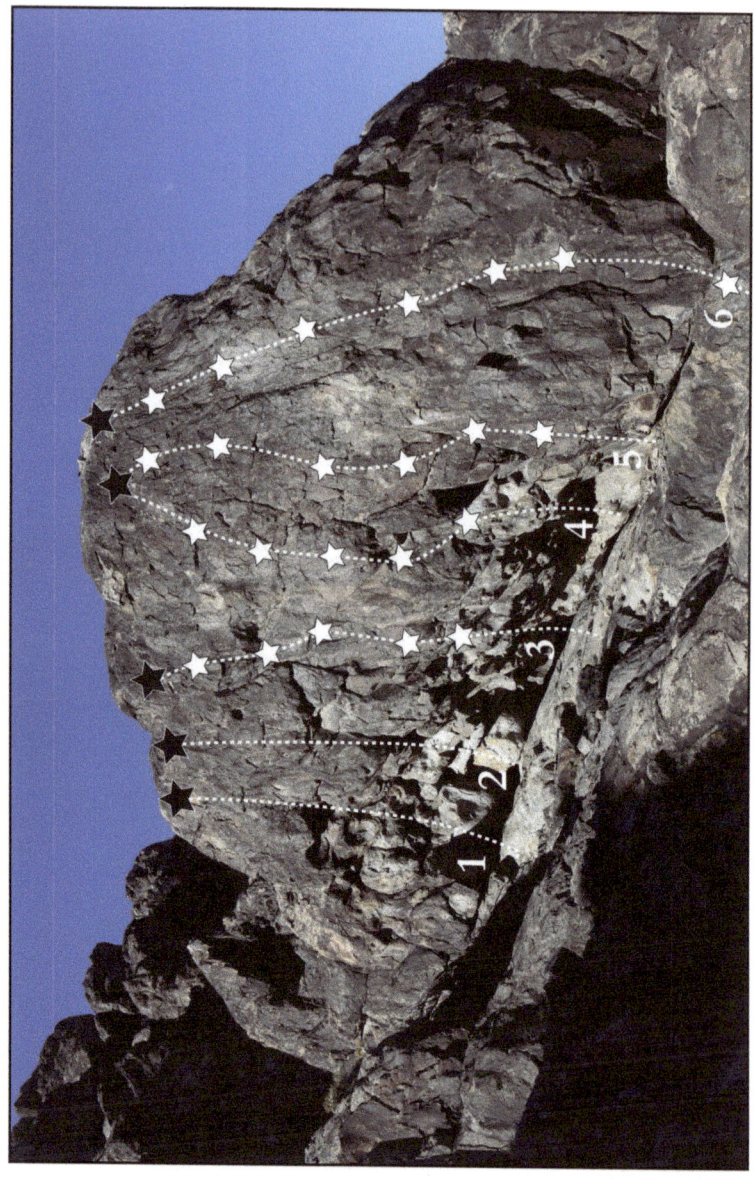

The Land That Time Forgot

Hidden Valley - North Wall

1. Project 1 (45')(Top Rope)
2. Project 2 (45')(Top Rope)

3. Cool To Be You 5.11d/12a (50')
Protection: 5 bolts, chain anchors

4. Stop Staring At My Ass ** 5.11b/c (55')
Protection: 5 bolts, chain anchors

5. Red Tape 5.10c (55')
Protection: 6 bolts, chain anchors

6. Technically Inept * 5.10a (55')**
Protection: 7 bolts, chain anchors

Sam Owings on Stop Staring at My Ass. Belayed by Snoop. (Right)

Dike Wall

The Land That Time Forgot

Dike Wall

Overview
Dike Wall is another previously undocumented crag. It sits on top of the ridge just north of Predator Wall. It is on the ridge-line east of the Big Horn Buttress and to the south. There is a large horizontal dike running across the face.

Approach
Same initial approach as Bighorn Buttress. As you enter the upper valley, follow the trail back south along the base of the valley. The trail will dead-end to some light scrambling east over the ridge-line to get to the Dike Wall formation. Walk around the big slab heading south to Dike Wall. It faces east.

Parking lot GPS: 34.665238, -116.984360

1. Lady In Red 5.11c (40')
Protection: 5 bolts, chain anchors

2. Black Jack 5.10b/c (40')
Protection: 6 bolts, chain anchors

West Canyon Crags

West Canyon Overview

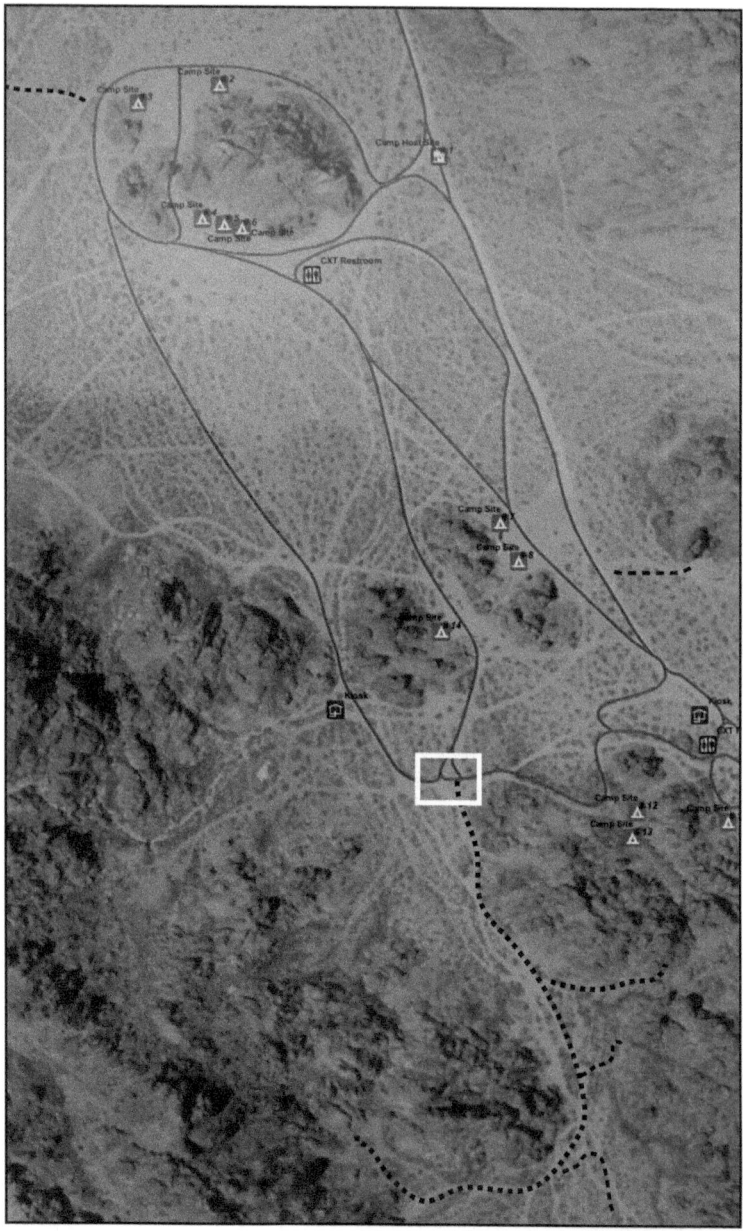

West Canyon Overview

Overview

The West Canyon was once home to off-road vehicles, open-range shooting, and broken bottles galore. Since the BLM development of Sawtooth Canyon Campground, all of the former dirt OHV (Off Highway Vehicle) roads have been closed off and reclaimed by nature. There are some remnants of the past still around, but most of it has been washed away. The west canyon has some excellent climbing. Most of it is around a 10-15-minute hike to get to with the old road system gone. The crowds have died down a little bit, but the classics still get the attention they deserve (Predator Wall, Dude Ranch, Watchtower). Trekking into the west canyon is definitely more of an adventure than it used to be. By New Jack City standards, all of the crags here are tucked away. If you don't know what to look for or where to go, crags can be easily missed.

Approach

Once you pass the main kiosk and then the Campground Host, take the road to the left of White Face at the fork. When you get to the vault toilet, make a left once you pass it, driving south and behind. Continue south, staying right at another fork until you reach a "T" intersection. You should see a dead-end parking area at the trail head for the west canyon (white box in left image).

Parking lot GPS: 34.666966, -116.982308

104   **West Canyon Crags**

West Canyon Crags

West Canyon Crags
Arch Rock

West Canyon Crags

Arch Rock

Overview

A dramatic natural arch formation, Arch rock has one of the most unique routes in the valley. Only a short walk from the West Canyon parking area, Arch Rock has three challenging routes. "The Travesty" is a real test of endurance and power. Climbing the full arch is the litmus test of New Jack City.

Approach

Take the main approach road for West Canyon. Park at the trail head and hike .17 miles along a washed-out road. Then head east up a gentle slope to get to Arch Rock (directly south of Club Butte).

GPS: 34.665254, -116.980987

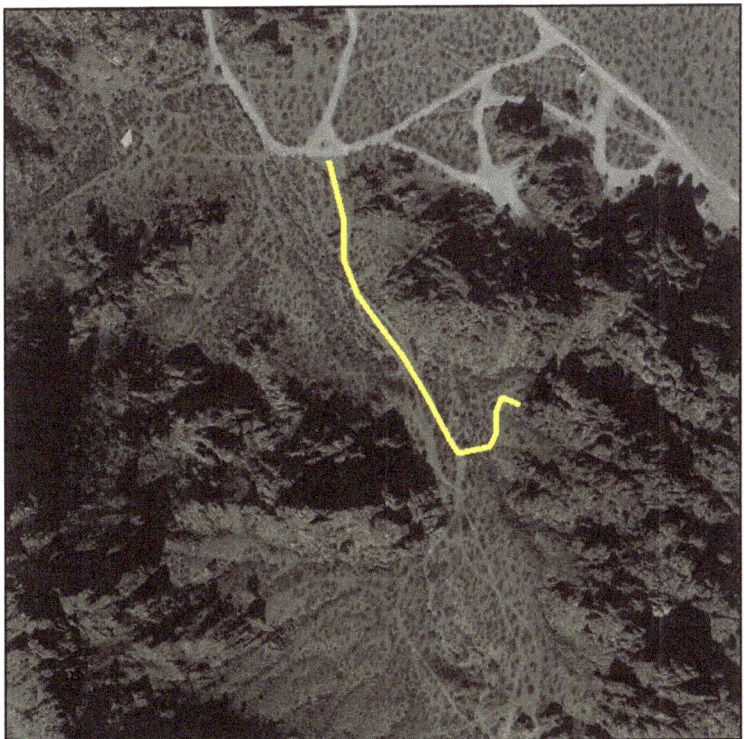

West Canyon Crags

Arch Rock

West Canyon Crags

Arch Rock

1. No Use for a Name ** 5.12b (40')
Around to the left of the main arch. A difficult short route with edges and a few pockets to get you past the main crux.
Protection: 4 bolts, shared chain anchors with Ride the Wild

2. Ride the Wild *** 5.12d (50')
To the right of No Use for a Name, a longer version with the same pockets. Throwing in some stretchy hand pulls and the usual overhanging moves, this takes it up a notch toward the Travesty.
Protection: 5 bolts, shared chain anchors with No Use for a Name

3. The Travesty **** 5.13a (30')
The main event, the Travesty is a short and challenging arch climb. Follow the main pillar up and take the overhanging traverse to the fifth bolt. From there, you have to make use of the minimal hands and feet to a final deadpoint to the sloper by the chains.
Protection: 6 bolts, chain anchors

West Canyon Crags

Club Blute

Overview
Club Blute is north of Arch Rock on the small ridge-line. There are a couple routes on quality rock put up by Bill 'Blitzo' Serniuk and Richard 'Locker' Thompson. The formation faces south and is in the sun year round.

Approach
Take the main approach road for West Canyon. Park at the trail head and hike .17 miles along an old washed-out road. Once you reach Arch Rock, take the trail north to Club Blute. You will see if from Arch Rock.

GPS: 34.666158, -116.980923

1. n00b Arete 5.7 (40')
Climb up the easy arete route left of the main bolted route.
Protection: top rope anchor and use the horn with a sling

2. Something borrowed something n00b 5.6 (40')
20' to first bolt. Face climb on varnished flakes to anchor on top.
Protection: 3 bolts, shut anchor and use a sling on the horn

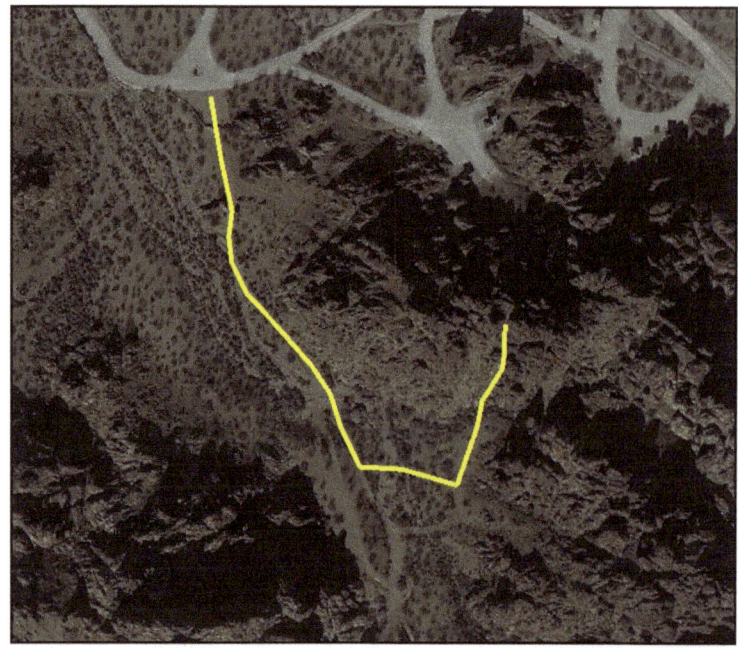

West Canyon Crags

Club Blute

Club Blute

West Canyon Crags 113

West Canyon

West Canyon Crags

Sunshine Face

West Canyon Crags

Sunshine Face

Overview
A great warm-up wall for Predator. On the right side of the washed-out road trail. Three moderate routes, in the sun all year.

Approach
Follow the trail from the West Canyon parking area toward Predator Wall. Just past the large boulder and when the trail turns west, Sunshine Face is up a small slope facing south.

GPS: 34.664983, -116.981742

1. Sunshine Superman * 5.10a (40')
A quick crux right at the first bolt. Take the left face to the top.
Protection: 3 bolts, shares anchors with Sunny Up

2. Sunny Up ** 5.9 (40')
Slightly easier version for Sunshine Superman. Decent face climb to the top.
Protection: 3 bolts, shares anchors with Sunshine Superman

3. Good Day Sunshine *** 5.10c (40')
Start to the right of the main face/soft arete. A variety of jugs, crimps, and good feet take you over a slight overhang.
Protection: 3 bolts, chain anchors

4. What's New Jack *** 5.10c (45') (not pictured)
Up the gully and on the north side of Sunshine Face.
Protection: 4 bolts, ring anchors

Liz Hurley Boulder

Overview
Just past the Sunshine Face is a great boulder problem. Liz Hurley is a fun, 20 foot problem with one closed-shut anchor on the top. Named after the hurling moves, this is an easily accessible problem with many other potential boulders around it.

Approach
Follow the trail from the West Canyon parking area toward Predator Wall. Take the trail west past Sunshine Face. Liz Hurley is north of the trail.

GPS: 34.664920, -116.982276

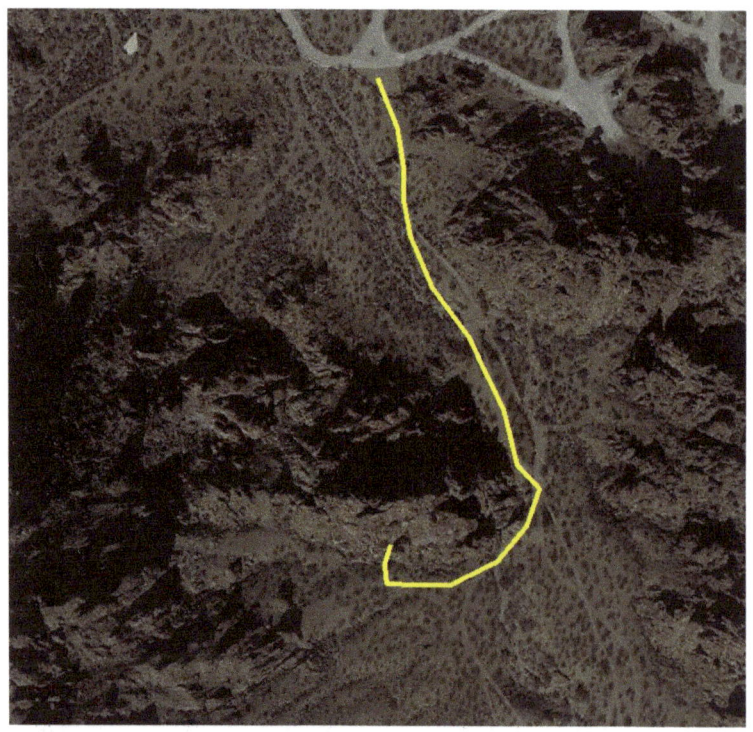

West Canyon Crags

Liz Hurley Boulder

Predator Wall

Predator Wall

Overview
The Predator Wall is the classic New Jack City monster crag. With routes from 5.10a through 5.12d, there's enough challenging stuff to go around. You now have to hike to the wall instead of driving and parking in front, so the crowds have slimmed down to the dedicated. Its one of the premier crags in the canyon and is challenging and long with a minimal approach.

Approach
Park at the West Canyon lot and take the old washed-out road south until the trail turns west. Angle your hike west up in to the canyon where Predator Wall resides. There is a well used trail that leads right up to the crag.

GPS: 34.664798, -116.983450

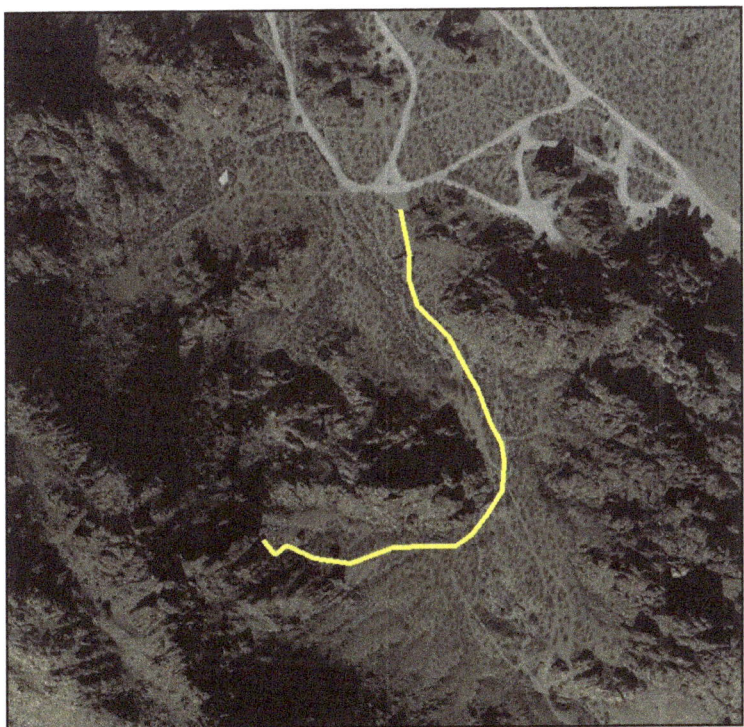

Predator Wall

West Canyon Crags

Predator Wall

Predator Wall

1. Straight Ahead 5.11b (40')
2. Rainbow Drive 5.11d (50')
3. Hallraker 5.12d (50')
4. Solitary Confinement 5.12a (40')
5. Body Scum 5.12b (40')
6. Sex Predator/Deviant 5.11b (40')
7. Sex Magik 5.12c (40')
8. The Predator 5.12c (50')
9. Crack in the Armor 5.12a (50')
10. Mental Block 5.12b (50')
11. Hero Worship 5.11b (50')
12. Vertigo 5.11a (50')
13. Combination Lock 5.12a (60')
14. This Nazi Shit Won't Do 5.11b (60')
15. Easy Prey 5.9 (60')
16. Bonus Fat 5.11b (60')
17. Central High 5.9 (60')

Predator Wall

1. Straight Ahead ** 5.11b (50')
Full stretch edges and crimps. Climb the bolt line.
Protection: 7 bolts, bolt anchors

2. Rainbow Drive * 5.11d (50')**
Boulder-like start to a first bolt crux. Moving up toward a dihedral with stemming, a few side pulls and a lie-back to make the top.
Protection: 6 bolts, shut anchors

Predator Wall

3. Hallraker **** 5.12d (50')
Overhanging start. Past the second bolt, look out for a kneebar and the crux is past the 4th bolt to the top. Super small edges on to better holds.
Protection: 7 bolts, shut anchors

4. Solitary Confinement *** 5.12a (40')
Technical start and some continuous difficulty make up this endurance route.
Protection: 6 bolts, shut anchors

West Canyon Crags 125

Predator Wall

Predator Wall

Previous Page Routes:
5. Body Scum ** 5.12b (40')
Boulder-like start to gain the first bolt. A stick clip may be necessary.
Protection: 6 bolts, shut anchors

6. Sex Predator/Deviant * 5.11b (40')**
A slightly overhanging route adds a bulge and some good holds up top.
Protection: 6 bolts, chain anchors

7. Sex Magik ** 5.12c (40')
A more challenging version of the Deviant. A variety of hand holds through the crux. Stretchy finish.
Protection: 6 bolts, chain anchors

8. The Predator * 5.12c (50')**
Follow the left side of the lower cave to the steep crux with some pumpy underclings and, if you're lucky, a knee bar.
Protection: 6 bolts, chain anchors

9. Crack in the Armor * 5.12b (50')**
Take the crack to the top of the cave. A technical and challenging climb.
Protection: 6 bolts, shut anchors

Routes pictured right
10. Mental Block ** 5.12b (50')
Follow the right-hand side of the cave. Crux at the first bolt. Hug the big block after the second bolt.
Protection: 5 bolts, chain anchors

11. Hero Worship * 5.11b (50')**
Steep slab climbing to a jug transition then on to more slab.
Protection: 6 bolts, shared chain anchors with Vertigo

12. Vertigo ** 5.11a (50')
Off-balance start. Cruise up the face and then veer right to top it off with a small crack and a relief jug before the anchors.
Protection: 6 bolts, shared chain anchors with Hero Worship

13. Combination Lock ** 5.12c (60')
Protection: 6 bolts, chain anchors

West Canyon Crags

Predator Wall

Predator Wall

14. This Nazi Shit Won't Do 5.11b (60')
Protection: 7 bolts, chain anchors

15. Easy Prey ** 5.9 (60')
A sustained, moderate climb on the side of the arete.
Protection: 7 bolts, chain anchors

16. Bonus Fat ** 5.11b (60')
Protection: 4 bolts, chain anchors

17. Central High 5.9 (60') (FA: Bruce Bindner)
Protection: 2 bolts, no anchors

West Canyon Crags

Predator Wall

Predator Wall - North Side

1. Red Tail Arete 5.12a (50')
2. Brown Recluse 5.11c/d (45')
3. One-Eyed Jack 5.10c (40')

West Canyon Crags

Predator Wall - North Side

4. Camp Stalker 5.10d (55')
5. Black Widow 5.11b (55')

Predator Wall - North Side

6. Crew of One 5.10b(40')

Predator Wall - North Side

1. Red Tail Arete ** 5.12a (50')
Protection: 5 bolts, chain anchor

2. Brown Recluse * 5.11c/d (45')**
Protection: 5 bolts, shut anchor

3. One Eyed Jack ** 5.10c (40')
Protection: 5 bolts, chain anchor

4. Camp Stalker ** 5.10d (55')
Protection: 6 bolts, chain anchor

5. Black Widow ** 5.11b (55')
Protection: 7 bolts, chain anchor

6. Crew of One 5.10b (40')
Protection: 4 bolts, chain anchor

Dude Ranch

West Canyon Crags

Dude Ranch

Overview
The Dude Ranch is visible from the West Canyon Parking lot. You can check to see how busy it is before walking out there. The Dude Ranch routes lean toward the more difficult range of the average climbing scale. It's a pretty short hike to get there, and you will find some rewarding routes. Slab, crack, chimney, huecos, the Dude Ranch is full of diverse features.

Approach
Starting from the West Canyon parking area, take the trail south to southeast for about .25 mile. The "Three Sisters" will be toward the southeast of the trail. Break off the main trail and head up the slope leading to a narrow crevice that you exit out of to the base of the Dude Ranch.

GPS: 34.664345, -116.980006

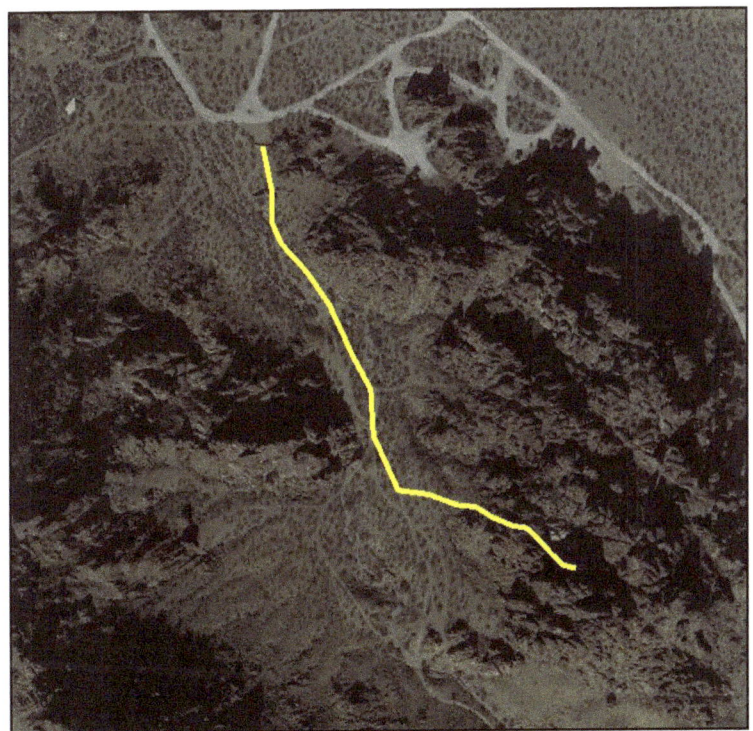

Upper Dude Ranch

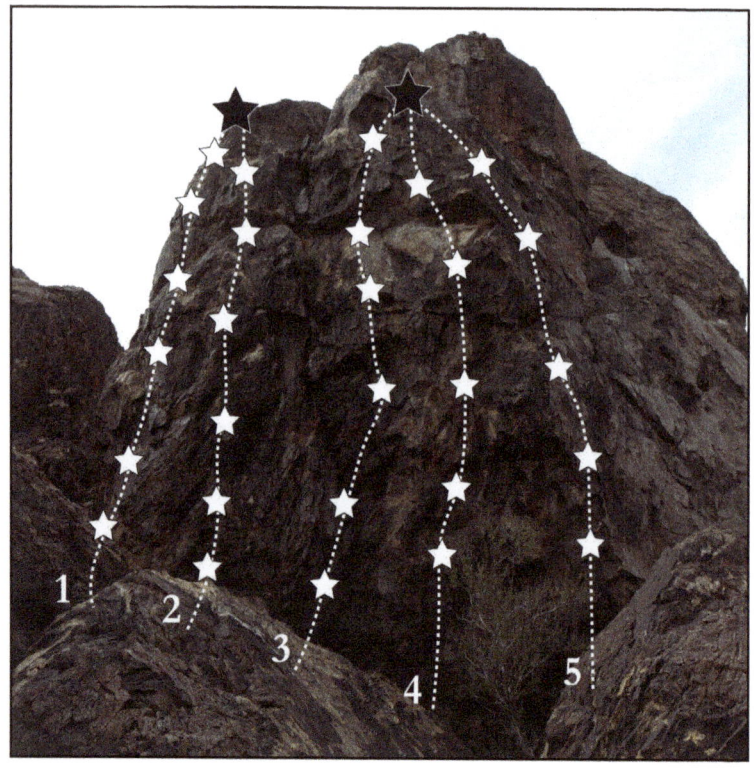

Upper Dude Ranch
1. **The Roundup 5.10b (40')**
2. **Getty-Up 5.11a (40')**
3. **Roughneck 5.11a (45')**
4. **Cromag 5.12a (45')**
5. **Celebate Rifle 5.10b (45')**

Upper Dude Ranch

Upper Dude Ranch

1. The Roundup ** 5.10b (40')
Far left route of Upper Ranch. Scramble up the gully up and around left of Lower Ranch. Shares anchors with Getty-Up. Well-protected and a standout for its rating.
Protection: 7 bolts, shared shut anchors

2. Getty-Up ** 5.11a (40')
The overhanging second route from the left. Difficult boulder-like start that mellows out slightly through to the top. Shares anchors with The Roundup.
Protection: 6 bolts, shared shut anchors

3. Roughneck *** 5.11a (45')
Similar start to Getty-Up but with a different take on the start. Shares anchors with and just to the left of Cromag.
Protection: bolts, shared shut anchors

4. Cromag *** 5.12a (45')
High first clip which is also the crux. Shares anchors with Roughneck
Protection: bolts, shared shut anchors

5. Celebate Rifle ** 5.10b (45')
In between Upper and Lower Ranch. Starts on the arete.
Protection: bolts, shared shut anchors

Lower Dude Ranch

Lower Dude Ranch
6. Funny Face 5.11a (50')
7. The Flake 5.10a (50')
8. Offwidth 5.11d (50') (No Protection)
9. Hidden Agenda 5.11c (75')
10. Voyeur 5.11a (75')
11. Unbolted Chimney (75')(No Pro)

12. City Slicker 5.10a (65')
13. Curly 5.10b (50')
14. Redneck 5.8 (50')

West Canyon Crags

Lower Dude Ranch

Lower Dude Ranch
6. Funny Face * 5.11a (50')**
Far left route of Lower Ranch. Scramble up the gully to a nice belay pad before the boulder that separates Upper and Lower. Somewhat sketchy start to the first clip. Fun with a variety of moves approaching the top.
Protection: 4 bolts, shut anchors

7. The Flake ** 5.10a (50')
Halfway up the gully to Funny Face. A high first clip with a punishing fall if missed. Might want to bring a crash pad or stick-clip.
Protection: 5 bolts, shut anchors

8. Offwidth 5.11d (50') (No protection)
Offwidth chimney with no protection. Just here for reference.
Protection: None

9. Hidden Agenda ** 5.11c (75')**
A standout for the crag. Face climb to reach the crux. Look for a kneebar to help out. Shares anchors and top three bolts with Voyeur.
Protection: 8 bolts, shared shut anchors

10. Voyeur ** 5.11a (75')
Harder side of the face and shares the top three bolts with Hidden Agenda
Protection: 7 bolts, shut anchor

11. Unbolted Chimney (75')(No Protection)

12. City Slicker ** 5.10a (50')
Follows the dihedral to shares anchors with Curly and Redneck.
Protection: 5 bolts, shut anchor

13. Curly * 5.10d (50')
Challenging slab to face climbing to reach the shared anchor.
Protection: 6 bolts, shut anchor

14. Redneck ** 5.8 (50')
Red rock face climb with lots of features. Shares anchors with Curly.
Protection: 6 bolts, shut anchor

Beyond Dude Ranch

Beyond Dude Ranch

Overview
This crag is directly across the huge boulders, east of Upper Dude Ranch. Two challenging routes share anchors at the top. Previously undocumented and thoroughly cleaned in winter of 2015.

Approach
Same approach as Upper Dude Ranch. Scramble up the big boulder on the left side of the Dude Ranch to reach Upper Dude Ranch. You will see Beyond Dude Crag, due east.

GPS: 34.664362, -116.979518

1. Been to the Edge 5.11d (50')
Protection: 6 bolts, shared shut anchors

2. Lost Your Edge 5.11c (50')
Protection: 5 bolts, shared shut anchors

West Canyon Crags

Toy Block

West Canyon Crags

Toy Block

Overview
The Toy Block is behind and below The Dude Ranch. There are three routes on perfect rock. Previously undocumented. Facing north, it's always in the shade.

Approach
Starting from the West Canyon parking area, take the trail south to southeast for about .25 mile. It's an easy trail on level ground. Go past The Dude Ranch and on its back side (south) and below is The Toy Block.

GPS: 34.664190, -116.980316

1. Woody 5.9 (40')
Protection: 4 bolts, chain anchors

2. Buzz 5.10b (40')
Protection: 4 bolts, shared chain anchors

3. To Infinity and Beyond 5.11b (40')
Protection: 4 bolts, shared chain anchors

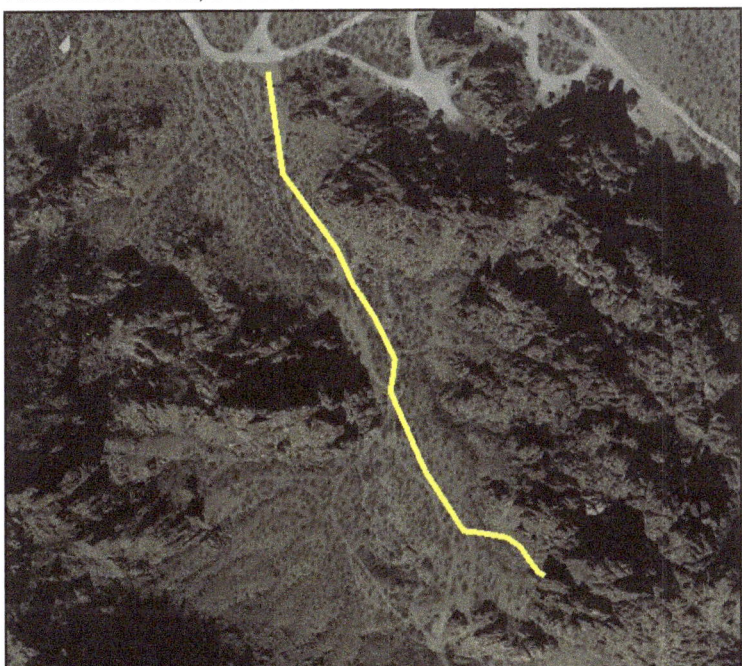

Korean Wall

West Canyon Crags

Korean Wall

Overview
There are three routes here with excellent rock quality. A lot of interesting features and varied climbing moves. The wall faces north. Also known as Granpa Simson.

Approach
Starting from the West Canyon parking area, take the trail south to southeast for about .5 mile. The trail becomes pretty washed-out as you get further south. Once the trail goes over the hill, you will be able to see the crag ahead. Walk up the gentle slope to reach the base of the crag.

GPS: 34.662972, -116.980246

1. Korean Wall Route 1 5.7 (35')
Protection: 3 bolts, hangers only, walk off back side.

2. Korean Wall Route 2 5.9+ (50')
Protection: 6 bolts, shared chain anchors

3. Korean Wall Route 3 5.11b (50')
Protection: 6 bolts, shared chain anchors

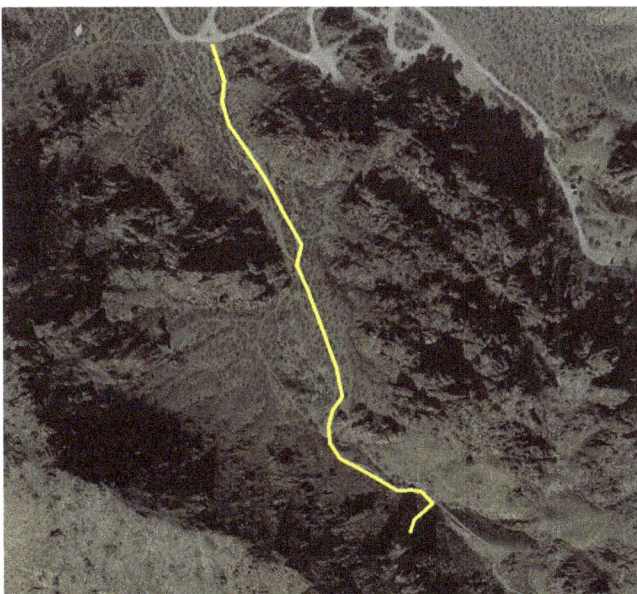

Cliffs of Insanity

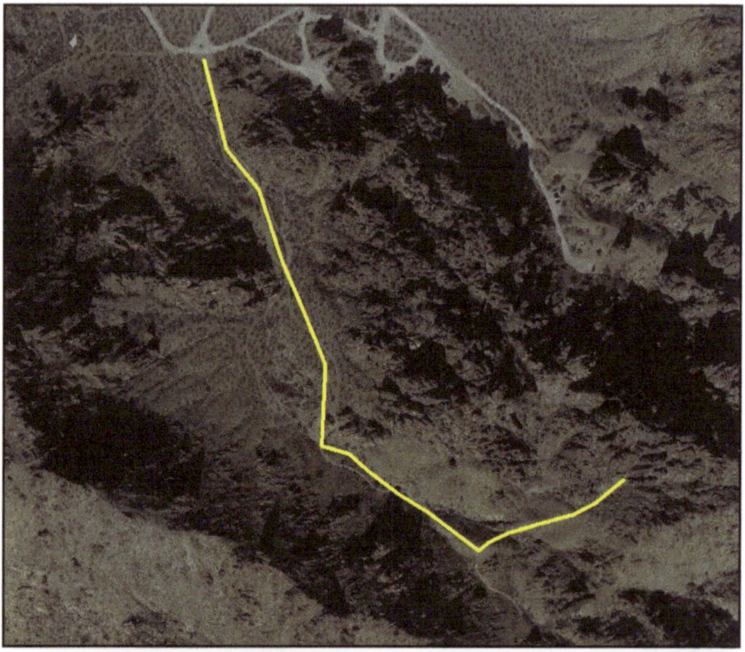

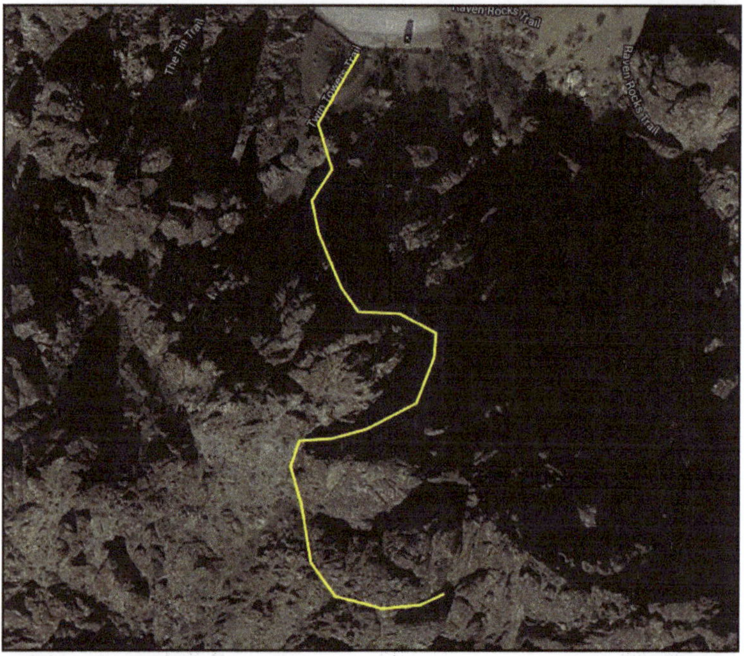

West Canyon Crags

Cliffs of Insanity

Overview
Moderate and long, the Cliffs of Insanity has the only multi-pitch routes in New Jack City. Also home to The Watchtower (The Action 13a) and the DX the Cliffs of Insanity stays sunny all year round.

Approach from West Canyon parking
Starting from the West Canyon parking area, take the trail south to southeast for about .5 mile. The trail becomes pretty washed-out as you get further south. Once the trail goes over the hill, you will be able to see the crag ahead. Keep following the trail south until you reach the big parking pad. Look for a feint trail that goes down the hill at an angle. There is a trail leading to the DX. Watch for cairns and take an uphill zig zag to the Scott Cosgrove Memorial Buttress.

Approach from East Canyon parking
From the main canyon parking area walk up past Slab City on its left side and hug the formation scrambling up the gully. You'll reach a big slabby face at the top. Head west here and continue over the ridge. As it slopes downhill to the West Canyon, hug the formation on the left as it curves southward. There is one small scramble up to the beginning of the Scott Cosgrove Memorial Buttress. Continue past to the main wall and more.

GPS: 34.663742, -116.978054

Scott Cosgrove Memorial Buttress

Overview
The first wall as you reach the Cliffs of Insanity. Varying degrees of difficulty and style. Deditcated to Scott Cosgrove (1964-2016). Developed by Geoff Fullerton, Scott Cosgrove, Jack Marshall, and Sam Owings. Route 1 starts on the ground on the southwest side of the buttress, 20 feet left of the scramble start. Top out on route 1 or scramble to reach routes 2-4. Rap links to get back down. Routes 5-6 start on the ground.

1. It Puts the Lotion on its Skin 5.7 (40')
Protection: 4 bolts, open shut anchors

2. Bombs Away 5.9 (65')
Protection: 6 bolts, open shut anchors

3. Dita's Play House 5.9+ (75')
Protection: 8 bolts, ring anchors

West Canyon Crags

Scott Cosgrove Memorial Buttress

4. Kestrel Dihedral 5.7 (85')
Fun dihedral to the summit.
Protection: 8 bolts, ring anchors

Scott Cosgrove Memorial Buttress

5. 1964 5.11+ (90')
Protection: 10 bolts, unfinished with sling

6. 2016 5.11+ (90')
Protection: 8 bolts, chain anchors

7. The DX 5.13a (70')
Protection: 10 chain draws, 2 chain draws anchor

Cosgrove Wall

Overview
Scramble up the large boulder leading to this upper level behind the DX. Developed by Scott Cosgrove.

8. Cosgrove Tower 5.10+ (75')
Start at the base of the tree and scramble up to the first bolt.
Protection: 7 bolts, chain anchors

Hidden Grotto

Overview
Scramble up the large boulder leading to this upper level behind the DX. This wall is in front and east of the back single-route wall.

9. Hidden Grotto Left 5.9 (45')
Short, fun with lots of features.
Protection: 4 bolts, chain anchors

10. Hidden Grotto Right 5.10a/b (45')
Fun climb with a crux move after the second bolt. High mantle to a long reach.
Protection: 4 bolts, chain anchors

West Canyon Crags

Hidden Grotto

West Canyon Crags

Cliffs of Insanity

Overview
This large west-facing cliff is well over 100'. The Cliffs of Insanity has the only two "multi-pitch" routes in New Jack City. Continue past the DX up the gully to the right (going southeast) to reach the base of these routes. These routes are great beginner multi-pitch routes.

All routes developed by Geoff Fullerton. These are excellent moderate routes with amazing views of the valley and the back side of the San Bernardino mountain range. Full afternoon sun year round.

11. Destination Oblivion 5.9 (60')
Access from ramp leading from routes 6 and 7. Rings for rappelling down. Very exposed and some loose rock off the bolt line.
Protection: 5 bolts, 3 open-shut anchors

12. Mostly Dead ** 5.8 (105')
Single pitch with a 70m. Long, fun, and really exposed. Excellent route for the grade.
Protection: 10 bolts, 3 open-shut anchors

13. Inconceivable *** 5.8 (120')
Can be done in a single pitch with a 70m and lower to the ground with rope stretch. For a 60m rope, lower to the rings and rap down. A couple commiting moves toward the last third of the pitch.
Protection: 3 bolts to belay station, 9 bolts to 3 open-shut anchors

14. Uncle Funs Basement *** 5.7 (120')
Can be done in a single pitch with a 70m and lower to the ground with rope stretch. Otherwise lower to the rings and rap down. Go right after the belay rings and up a really juggy and fun route.
Protection: 3 bolts to belay station, 7 bolts to 3 open-shut anchors

15. Red Headed She Devil 5.10+ (70')
Scramble up the gully from the main belay notch. Just left of The Action
Protection: 8 bolts, chain anchors

Cliffs of Insanity

The Watchtower

Overview

The Watchtower, home to the iconic route, The Action, overlooks the West Canyon area and into the Stoddard Valley. From the top of the crag, you can also see down into the East Canyon to Raven Rocks. Scramble up from the Cliffs of Insanity belay notch to the upper gully to reach The Watchtower.

1. The Action **** 5.13a (60')
This is the iconic, difficult, sustained overhanging route of New Jack City.
Protection: 9 Bolts, chain anchors

2. Watchtower Direct * 5.11a (75')
To the right of The Action is the easier of the two routes on the Watchtower.
Protection: 5 bolts, chain anchors

The Watchtower

Fullerton Wall - South

Overview
Below and just south of The Watchtower is the second Geoff Fullerton formation. There are four routes. Either walk down and around south to access or scramble up to the ridge-line, veer south, then follow the gully to route 4.

GPS: 34.663532, -116.977628

16. Toe Tag ** 5.8 (45')
Protection: 5 bolts, open shuts

17. The Crawl Space ** 5.9 (45')
Protection: 4 bolts, open shuts

18. The 4 Horsemen ** 5.11a (55')**
Don't pull outward on the dinner plate-like feature.
Protection: 6 bolts, open shuts

19. Bog of Eternal Stench 5.11b/c (55')
Protection: 4 bolts, mussy hook anchors

Fullerton Wall - South

East Canyon Crags

Overview

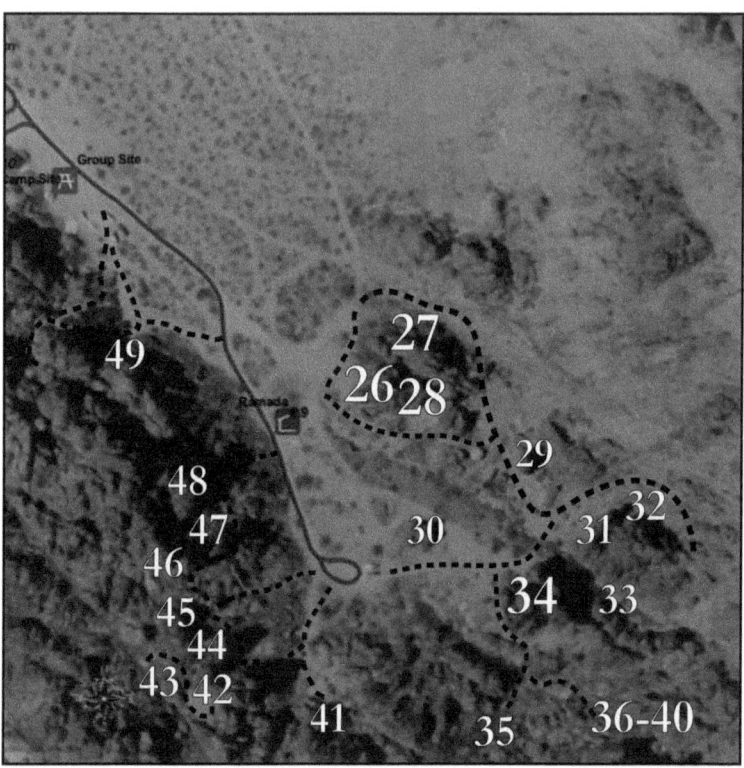

26. Parking Lot Rock	Page	175
27. Hidden Wall	Page	177
28. Sunnyside Crag	Page	179
29. Hueco Wall	Page	183
30. The Pinnacle	Page	189
31. Crucified Crag	Page	193
32. Beyond the Crucified	Page	197
33. Indirect Crag	Page	199
34. Raven Rocks	Page	201
35. The Getaway	Page	229
36. Raven's Roost	Page	236
37. The Shreen	Page	237

East Canyon Crags

Overview

38. Nose Wall	Page	238
39. Fantasy Island	Page	239
40. The Fairway	Page	243
41. Hard Rock Cafe/Slab City	Page	249
42. The Finger	Page	253
43. Prodigy Pile	Page	255
44. Twin Towers	Page	257
45. Pat & Jack's Pinnacle	Page	263
46. Lethal Rock	Page	267
47. The Fin	Page	271
48. Crossfire Crag	Page	273
49. Boy Scout Wall	Page	281

East Canyon Crags

Overview

East Canyon Crags

Overview

Overview

The east canyon is the main event of New Jack City. You'll find the most crowds here due to the diverse range of climbs and the minimal to zero approach. There are the classics like Raven Rocks, The Finger, Crossfire Crag, etc. There are 23 crags, which means there is something for everyone, and that's why everyone's here!

Approach

As you approach the campground host, the road will veer to the right and come to a fork. Make a left and stay to the left until you reach the end of the road. This is where the main parking area is (pictured two pages back). If everyone is efficient, you can get about 16 cars up there. The next parking "lot" back is by Parking Lot Crag (park head-in to the fence, facing south). After that, there are a few spots here and there. On busy days, be prepared to walk in from the entrance area crags. Please be respectful of the campground parking spots since they are reserved for the occupants.

Main Parking Area
GPS: 34.665226, -116.978086

Parking locations below:

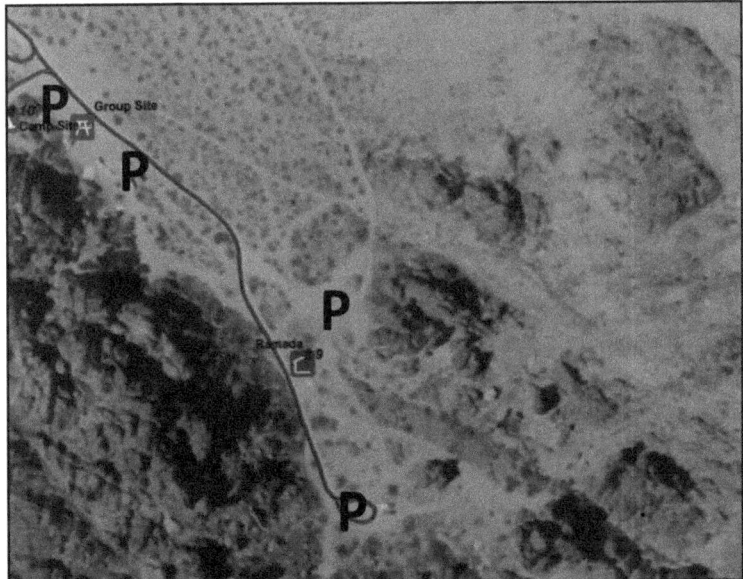

166 East Canyon Crags

East Canyon Crags

Overview

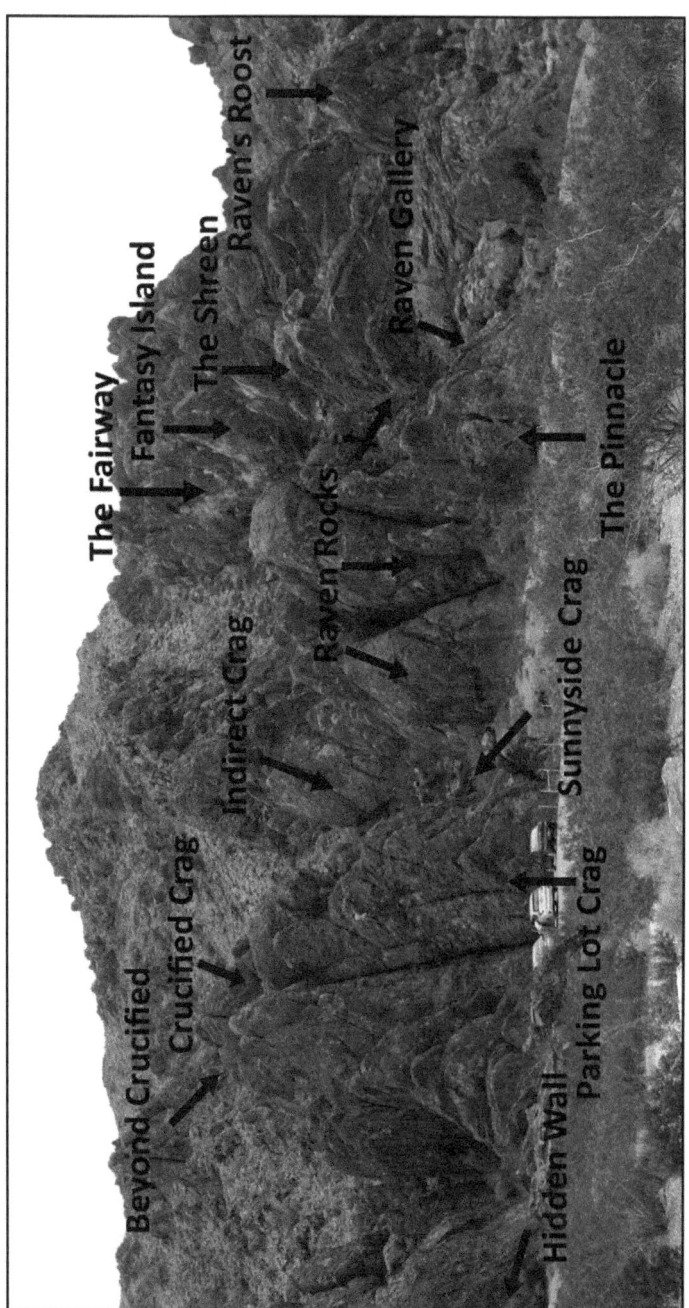

East Canyon Crags

Overview

Overview

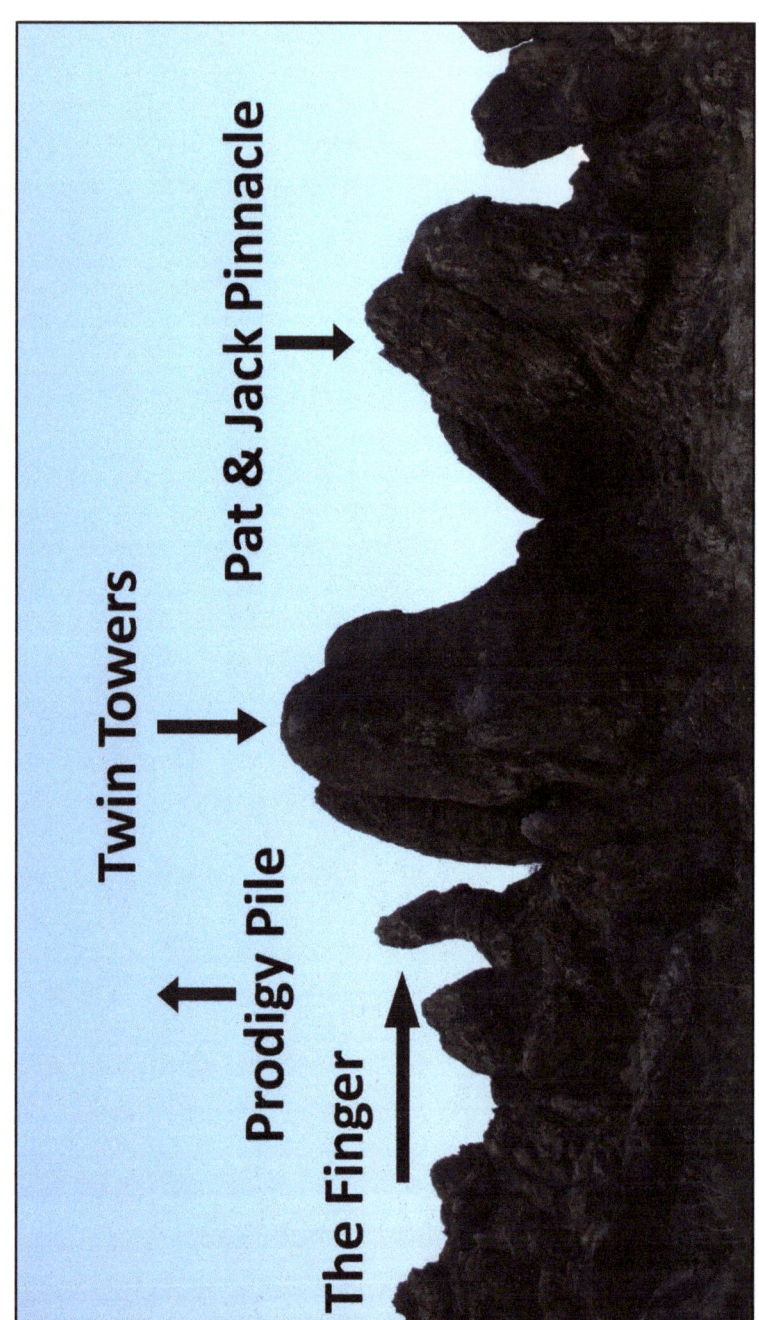

Overview

172 East Canyon Crags

Busy day at Sunnyside Face

East Canyon Crags 173

Sender One youth team on Raven Rocks West

Parking Lot Rock

East Canyon Crags

Parking Lot Rock

Overview
Parking Lot Rock is the west face of the Sunnyside/Hidden Wall/Parking Lot formation. As you can see in the topo picture, you can almost belay from your car. There is only one route here, and it's the secondary parking area for the East Canyon.

Approach
As you approach the campground host, the road will veer to the right and come to a fork. Make a left and stay to the left until you see a turn off on the left that goes up a small hill to a large, uneven parking pad in front of Parking Lot Rock.

GPS: 34.666046, -116.978154

1. Little Jack Horner * 5.6 (35')
A short and fun 5.6 with plenty of holds and comfortable protection for beginners. Lots of angled underclinging holds. Crux is just after the 4th bolt.
Protection: 4 Bolts, chain anchors

Hidden Wall

East Canyon Crags

Hidden Wall

Overview
Hidden Wall is the north side of the Sunnyside/HiddenWall/Parking Lot formation. There are five moderately difficult routes and plenty of shade in the afternoon.

Approach
Same approach as Parking Lot Rock. Walk around to the left (north) of Parking Lot Rock. Hidden Wall is the north-facing side of the formation. There is a well-worn trail.

GPS: 34.666153, -116.977735

1. Back from the Dead *** 5.12a (35')
A variety of holds and tricky moves make up this short but challenging route. Starting at the bottom, it wanders up and to the right on the steep left side of the crag.
Protection: 5 bolts, chain anchors

2. Six Pack ** 5.11d (35')
Start below the big scoop and move up on easier moves to a difficult finish at the anchors.
Protection: 5 bolts, chain anchors

3. King of all Media *** 5.11d (35')
Underclings, side pulls, and technical foot moves. Follow the crack to the top.
Protection: 5 bolts, ring anchors

4. Let's Kung Fu ** 5.12c (35')
Climb up and out of the cave to small hand holds on the face climb finish.
Protection: 5 bolts, chain anchors

5. Backside Arete *** 5.11d (35')
Follow the arete on the side of the cave up to the crux. Small feet and crimps up to the anchors.
Protection: 5 bolts, chain anchors

6. Gut Reaction 5.11a (35')
Protection: 4 bolts, shut anchors

East Canyon Crags

Sunnyside Wall

East Canyon Crags

Sunnyside Wall

Overview
Sunnyside Wall is on the south-facing side of the Sunnyside/Hidden Wall/Parking Lot formation. There are eight relatively easier routes that are in the sun almost all day. Routes range from 5.7-5.10 with a .12 thrown in.

Approach
Same initial approach as Parking Lot Rock. Walk around to the right (south) of Parking Lot Rock. Sunnyside Wall is the south-facing side of the formation. The first small gully has two 5.7s. The other routes are on the main wall.

GPS: 34.665884, -116.978012

Sunnyside Wall

1. Cheap Lipstick 5.7 (30')
2. Powder Puff 5.7 (30')
3. Chick Flaky 5.10c (60')
4. Fun in the Sun 5.9 (45')

Sunnyside Wall

5. Red Hot 5.12a (40')
6. Dr. Know 5.10b (40')
7. Goldfinger 5.10a (45')
8. Walk in the Park 5.7 (45')

Sunnyside Wall

1. Cheap Lipstick ** 5.7 (30')
The short and fun twin of Powder Puff. Another easy beginner lead. Shares anchors with Powder Puff and in the same gully. Dusty belay area.
Protection: 6 bolts, shared ring anchor

2. Powder Puff ** 5.7 (30')
Fun and short, a great easy lead and always in the sun. High first bolt but very easy climbing. Shares anchors with Cheap Lipstick. In a small gully with a dusty belay area.
Protection: 3 bolts, shared ring anchor

3. Chick Flaky * 5.10c (60')**
Boulder-like start that is protected on to a well marked flake. Small foot holds toward the top.
Protection: 7 bolts, chain anchors

4. Fun in the Sun ** 5.9 (45')
A great dihedral that follows right of the ledge of Chick Flaky.
Protection: 6 bolts, shut anchors

5. Red Hot ** 5.12a (40')
Difficult start to a very hard second clip. For shorter climbers, be aware of the reachy third clip.
Protection: 5 bolts, clip in anchors (gym type)

6. Dr. Know ** 5.10b (40')
Difficult for the grade but with a clear line. Awkward and balancy climbing.
Protection: 4 bolts, shut anchors

7. Goldfinger * 5.10a (45')
A fun route with positive holds and a vertical south-facing line.
Protection: 5 bolts, chain anchors

8. Walk in the Park * 5.8 (45')
A fun, well-protected route on the far right of the wall. A lot of good holds with somewhat obvious foot placement.
Protection: 6 bolts, chain anchors

East Canyon Crags

Hueco Wall

Hueco Wall

Overview

Hueco Wall has excellent rock quality and outstanding features. It mostly faces west and south, and all routes are in the 5.10-5.11 range. It is the 45' spire in between Raven Rocks and Sunnyside. There's a handmade cement rock bench at the base of the arete for some comfortable belaying.

Approach

From the main parking area, follow the trail toward Raven Rocks and veer left at the top of the initial hill. Directly across from Raven Rocks North is a trail that leads down into a small wash and back up the other side. Hueco Wall should be right in front of you. Walk across some rocks to reach the base. Its hard to miss and the trails are obvious.

GPS: 34.665627, -116.977280

Hueco Wall - East Face

Hueco Wall - West Face

1. Bitter End 5.10c (40')(previous page)
2. They All Look the Same 5.10d (40')
3. Good to be Awake 5.11b (50')
4. Gun for Hire 5.11b (50')
5. Sluttering 5.11a (50')

Hueco Wall - South Face

6. Room for Improvement 5.10d (45')
7. Sex Dance 5.11b (40')
8. Dance This 5.11a (40')
9. Ryane's Revenge 5.10a (35')

Hueco Wall

1. Bitter End * 5.10c (40')**
Protection: 4 bolts, chain anchors

2. They All Look the Same ** 5.11d (40')
A good sequence of moves that winds back and forth across the bolt line.
Protection: 5 bolts, shut anchor

3. Good to be Awake * 5.11b (50')**
Technical with small crimps up the face.
Protection: 6 bolts, chain anchors

4. Gun for Hire * 5.11b (50')**
Vertical to overhanging climb using a mix of crimps and huecos.
Protection: 7 bolts, shut anchors

5. Sluttering ** 5.11a (50')
Climb up the arete to a high crux finish.
Protection: 5 bolts, chain anchors

6. Room for Improvement * 5.10d (45')**
Climb up the short ramp and move up onto the face. A small roof crux awaits toward the top.
Protection: 5 bolts, chain anchors

7. Sex Dance ** 5.11b (40')
A slight variation to Dance This. A boulder-like start is the crux, then on to finish with Dance This.
Protection: 6 bolts, shared chain anchors

8. Dance This ** 5.11a (40')
Face climbing to start then toward a crux with crimps. It gets a bit steep toward the top.
Protection: 6 bolts, shared chain anchors

9. Ryane's Revenge ** 5.10a (35')
Easiest route on the Hueco Wall. Fun and solid moves up the face.
Protection: 4 bolts, chain anchors

East Canyon Crags

The Pinnacle

The Pinnacle - East Face

Overview
The Pinnacle is the middle formation you pass on the left while walking toward Raven Rocks. There are two short routes on the east face.

Approach
From the main parking area, you'll see The Pinnacle up the small hill and to the north of the main path.

GPS: 34.665386, -116.977745

1. The Pups Are Doggin' It 5.11a (30')
Protection: 3 bolts, shared chain anchors

2. Sophie's Choice * 5.10a (30')
Protection: 3 bolts, shared chain anchors

The Pinnacle - North Face

3. La Fissura 5.9 (30')
Protection: 3 bolts, chain anchors

4. What The...* 5.10a (30')
Protection: 4 bolts, chain anchors

Crucified Crag

East Canyon Crags 193

Crucified Crag

Overview
Crucified Crag is east of Hueco Wall and northeast of Raven Rocks. A north-facing wall provides shade most of the day.

Approach
From the main parking lot, take the main path up toward Raven Rocks. Take the Hueco Wall trail into the wash and then take the fork to the right. Crucified Crag is the large wall with a tower on the left.

GPS: 34.665503, -116.976861

1. **Crucified 5.11b (65')**
2. **Life Returns 5.11a (70')**
3. **One More Victim 5.11b (80')**
4. **From the Ashes 5.10d (80')**
5. **Sundowner 5.10c (80')**
6. **Demolition Man 5.10d (80')**
7. **Another Piece of Meat 5.10b (50')**

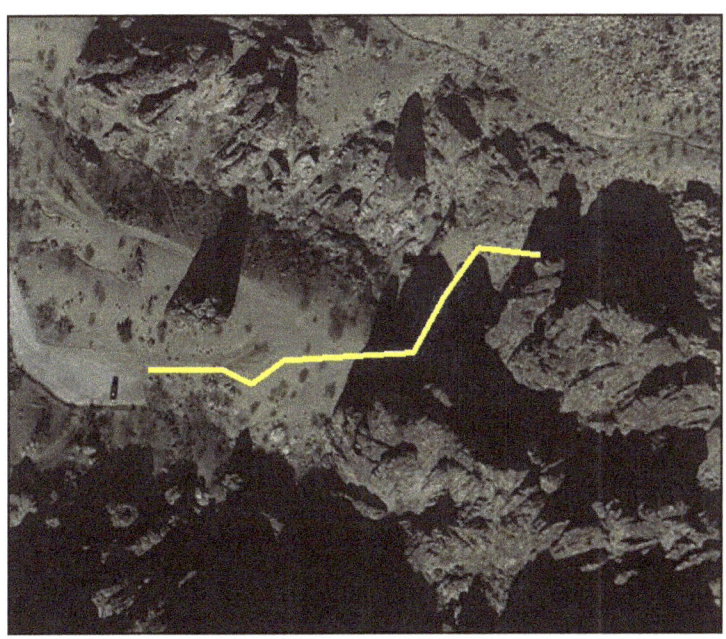

Crucified Crag

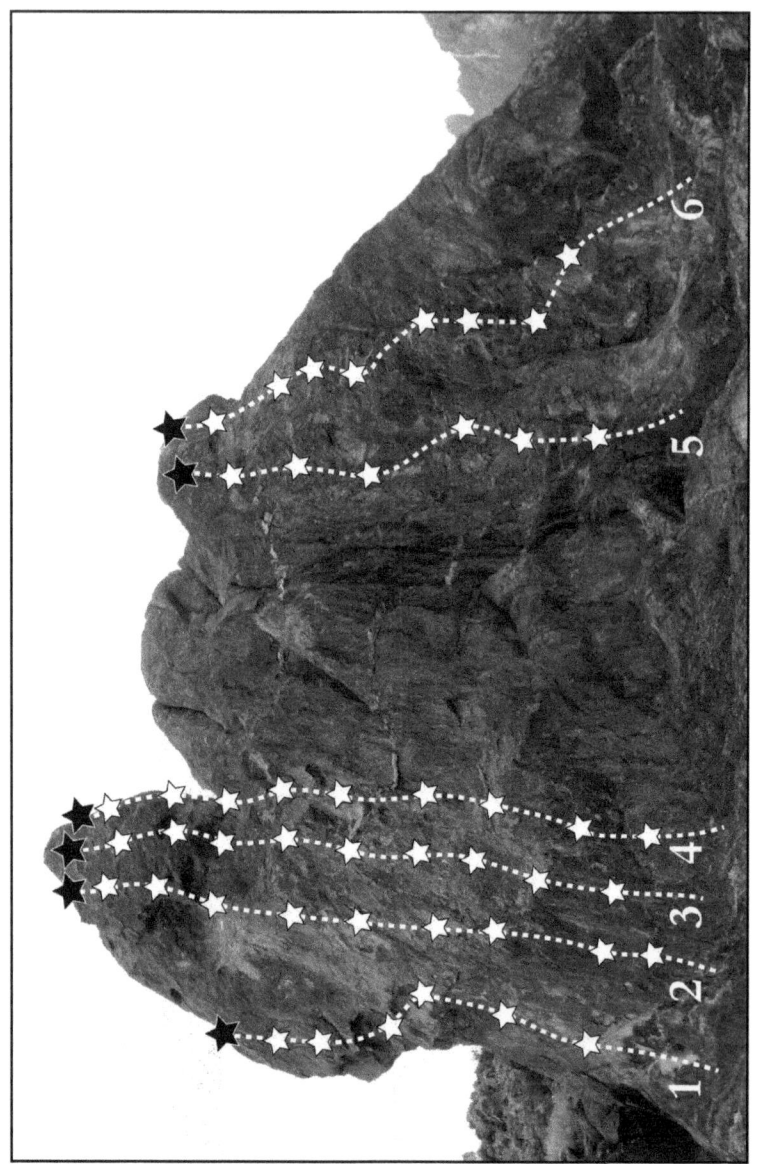

East Canyon Crags

Crucified Crag

Crucified Crag

1. Crucified 5.11b (65')
A classic. Tricky face climbing up through a scoop on the wall. A variety of awkward holds and fun climbing overall.
Protection: 6 bolts, chain anchors

2. Life Returns 5.11a (70')
A slight variation of Crucified with the cruxes being inside, and out of the scoop. Small holds and feet through the face.
Protection: 9 bolts, chain anchors

3. One More Victim 5.11b (80')
Boulder-like start to easier climbing up to the overhanging top section.
Protection: 9 bolts, chain anchors

4. From the Ashes 5.10d (80')
A boulder-like start similar to One More Victim. Pass the roof to a steep finish.
Protection: 9 bolts, chain anchors

5. Sundowner 5.10c (80')
A crux in the middle with crimpy holds. Easier finish toward the top.
Protection: 6 bolts, chain anchors

6. Demolition Man 5.10d (80')
Long face climbing to a small bulge.
Protection: 8 bolts, chain anchors

7. Another Piece of Meat 5.10b (50')
Around the left side of the main tower, left of Crucified.
Protection: 5 bolts, shut anchors

Beyond The Crucified

Overview
Beyond Crucified is just up and around the left side of the main Crucified Crag. There are three more moderate routes that are mostly in the shade all year long.

Approach
Same approach as Crucified Crag. Continue east and around the main Crucified tower on your right. Go up a small hill to the belay ledge.

GPS: 34.665478, -116.976710

1. Rattle the Cattle * 5.7 (45')
Protection: 4 bolts, bolt anchors

2. Hale Bop Tango ** 5.8 (50')
Protection: 6 bolts, shared anchors

3. Beyond the Crucified ** 5.8 (55')
Protection: 6 bolts, shared anchors

Indirect Crag

East Canyon Crags

Indirect Crag

Overview
Indirect Crag is past the north side of Raven Rocks up a small gully. A handful of great routes in a shady gully. Indirect Action has two options for bolt lines.

Approach
Approach the same as Raven Rocks North. Continue past and around right of Raven Rocks and up a gully. There are two paths that reach this crag. Each on one side of the gully. The trails are well worn and easily followed. Belay spots are along the hill with a flatter spot on top for Back with a Bang.

GPS: 34.665117, -116.976891

1. Back with a Bang ** 5.12a (45')
A short, steep, and difficult route that climbs up a hueco-filled face. Use the last bolt on Walk the Talk to the shared anchors.
Protection: 5 bolts, shared chain anchors

2. Walk the Talk * 5.12c (50')**
A longer, yet similar route to Back with a Bang. A little steep with the same theme of holds. Shares its chain anchors with Back with a Bang.
Protection: 8 bolts, shared chain anchors

3. Indirect Action * 5.9 (70')**
Clip the third bolt up and to the left, then traverse left across two more bolts. Difficult to clean.
Protection: 8 bolts, chain anchors

4. 72 Hour Hold 5.9 (70')
Protection: 8 bolts, chain anchors

5. Working Men R Pissed 5.9 (35')
Protection: 4 bolts, chain anchors

Raven Rocks

Raven Rocks

Overview
Raven Rocks is a very popular multi-wall formation in the east canyon. It is separated into four sections named after the general direction to which each face points. There are 30 different routes that range from 5.7-5.13b. All sides of this formation see a lot of crowding.

Approach
From the parking lot at the end of the road, walk up the trail east to the west face of the Raven Rocks formation.

GPS: 34.665182, -116.977424

Raven Rocks East

East Canyon Crags

Raven Rocks East

Overview
The east and shady section of Raven Rocks has six routes ranging from 5.10a-5.12a.

Approach
From the parking lot at the end of the road, walk up the trail east to the west face of the Raven Rocks formation. Continue left and pass the cave on your right. The east face is behind the cave.

GPS: 34.665182, -116.977424

1. **Little Red Book 5.10a (80')**
2. **Unknown Route 5.10d (70')**
3. **Stop the Madness 5.12a (40')**
4. **Little Stiffy 5.11c (40')**
5. **Shaky Start 5.10d (70'**
6. **Balancing Act 5.10a (70')**

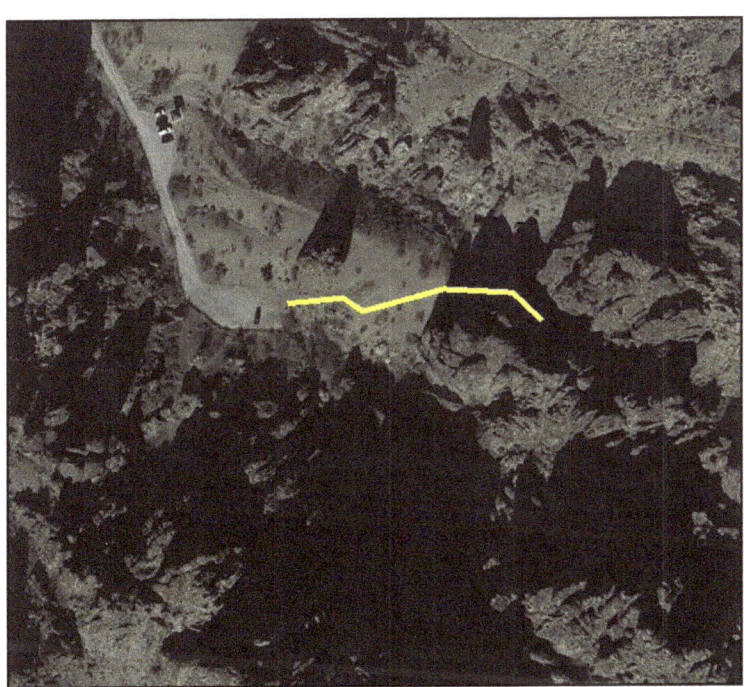

Raven Rocks East

1. Little Red Book * 5.10a (80')**
Climb up two corners over 8 bolts to reach the chain anchors.
Protection: 8 bolts, chain anchors

2. Punk Rock Changed Our Life 5.10d (70')
Just to the right of Little Red Book, left of Stop the Madness.
Protection: 6 bolts, chain anchors

3. Stop the Madness * 5.12a (40')**
Short but sustained endurance route across a variety of holds and technical feet.
Protection: 4 bolts, chain anchors

4. Little Stiffy * 5.11c (40')**
Climb up to a huge hueco and continue to the crux from steep to vertical.
Protection: 4 bolts, chain anchors

5. Shaky Start 5.10d (70')
Climb to the right of the arete next to Little Stiffy. Shares anchors with Balancing Act.
Protection: 6 bolts, chain anchors

6. Balancing Act 5.10a (70')
Take the off-width crack to an easier face climb. Shares anchors with Shaky Start.
Protection: 5 bolts, chain anchors

Raven Rocks North

Overview

Raven Rocks North (The Power Block) boasts 14 routes ranging from 5.10a to 5.13a. A lot of overhanging routes and a big cave like feature make up one of the largest concentration of higher grades. This area is just left of the west face. Red Devil was the first bolted route in New Jack City.

Approach

From the parking lot at the end of the road, walk up the trail heading east and continue left along Raven Rocks until you reach the big cave-like feature. The cave is in the middle of the Power Block

GPS: 34.665236, -116.977283

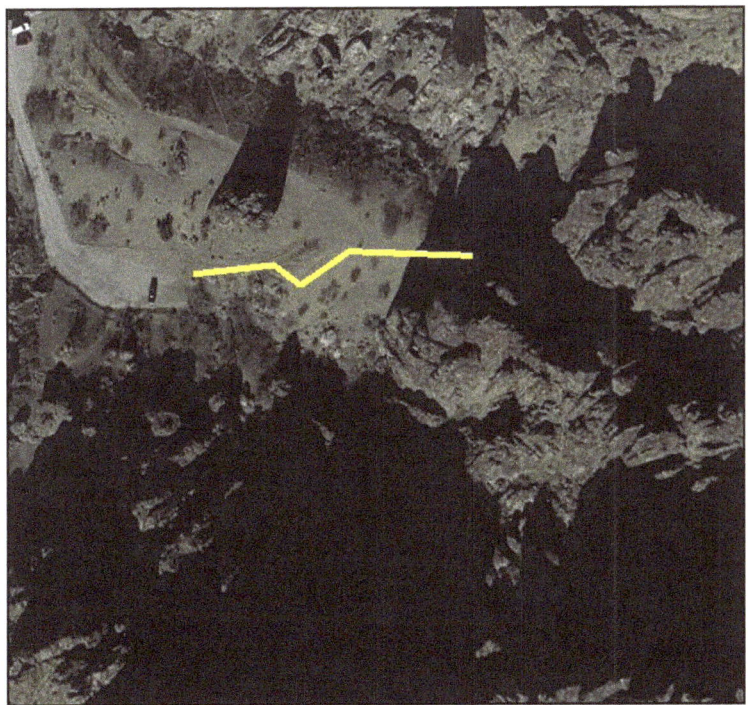

Raven Rocks North

Raven Rocks North

1. Voodoo Child *** 5.13b (50')
Start just right of Balancing Act and traverse to and link up with Disconnected's third bolt. Complete its crux and then move on toward the anchors of Voodoo Lounge. Use the last bolt and finish the Voodoo Lounge crux to the anchors.
Protection: 6 bolts, Voodoo Lounge's chain draw anchors

2. Disconnected ** 5.12c (45')
Boulder-like start that traverses left through the crux. Solid handholds but poor footholds.
Protection: 5 bolts, chain draws anchor

3. Voodoo Lounge *** 5.13a (35')
Climb up through the cave through a mini crux at the second bolt. A boulder-like crux-finish to the anchors.
Protection: 5 bolts, chain draws anchor

4. You Don't Know Jack **** 5.12c (35')
Boulder-like start with an optional leap to the high jug under the roof. Move toward the obvious chalked jug. Moving left, keep your balance to gain a lie-back and a decent flake above. Hard finishing moves to reach the anchor.
Protection: 4 draws, chain draw anchors

5. Red Devil *** 5.12b (35')
Boulder-like start with an optional leap to the high jug under the roof. Move toward the obvious chalked jug. Moving right, staying away from You Don't Know Jack draws to the Red Devil chain anchors.
This was the first bolted route in New Jack City.
Protection: 2 chain draws, 3 bolts, chain anchors

Raven Rocks North

East Canyon Crags

Raven Rocks North

6. Espresso *** 5.10c (35')
Well-protected face to overhanging climb. The transition above the cave is the crux.
Protection: 4 bolts, shut anchors

7. Decaf ** 5.10a (35')
A dihedral climb with crack options.
Protection: 4 bolts, chain anchors

Raven Rocks North

Raven Rocks North

8. Blast from the Past ** 5.11a (80')
Climb up the slab, clip the first bolt, and move across the chimney to the main wall. Climb up the face to the anchors at the headwall.
Protection: 8 bolts, chain anchors

9. Holy Moley * 5.10a (90')**
Huecos, huecos, huecos. Climb on to the face and over a bulge to the anchors. Shares anchors with The Raven.
Protection: 12 bolts, shared chain anchors

10. The Raven ** 5.11a (90')
Face climbing to a large hueco that comes out onto the crux. Long face climb to the shared anchors with Holy Moley. Stemming onto Should Be Called Do What is off route.
Protection: 9 bolts, shared chain anchors

11. Should Be Called Do What? ** 5.10c (80')
Climb up the main boulder face with crimps until you reach the top. Then bridge over to the main wall to more face climbing to reach the anchors.
Protection: 8 bolts, chain anchors

12. RepoMan * 5.10b (40')
Boulder-like start with underclings and side-pulls. Decent feet halfway up, then move onto a featured face to the anchors.
Protection: 4 bolts, shut anchors

Raven Rocks North

Raven Rocks North

13. Will Power ** 5.11a PG13 (30')
A short, challenging and balancy route. The first bolt is high, but has a good position to clip. Keep your nerves together and continue to the second bolt then anchors.
Protection: 2 bolts, chain anchors

14. Tough Choices ** 5.10c (35')
Boulder-like start to a balancy crux. Short and fun.
Protection: 3 bolts, shut anchors

Raven Rocks West

East Canyon Crags **215**

Raven Rocks West

Overview
The west face of Raven Rocks (aka Warm-up Wall) is home to 7 routes ranging from 5.9-5.11b. Good rock quality and an excellent belay area. Morning shade and mid-day and afternoon sun. Usually very busy and a little dusty beause of the traffic.

Approach
From the parking lot at the end of the road, walk up the trail heading east and walk straight to the main face and go right into the belay area for the west crag.

GPS: 34.665093, -116.977449

Raven Rocks West

East Canyon Crags

Raven Rocks West

1. Rob's Rambunctious Ride ** 5.9 (75')
Face climbing left of the bolt line. A less-than-vertical start to some fun exposure at the top. A cool hueco approaching the anchors. A fun, well-protected route.
Protection: 9 bolts, shut anchors

2. Same Same but Different ** 5.10c (65')
Varied movement with reachy handholds as you move toward the middle. Some technical moves to stay away from the crack (off route).
Protection: 7 bolts, shut anchors

3. Love Onsite* 5.10c (65')**
Balancy and stretchy moves through a well-protected route. The crux is toward the top as you reach the anchors.
Protection: 8 bolts, chain anchors

4. Welcome to New Jack City * 5.10a (60')**
Sustained, well-protected and greatly featured route. Truly deserving of the namesake, It's on display, front and center. Crux after the last bolt to a long reach past the anchors.
Protection: 6 bolts, shut anchors

5. Step Across * 5.10a (85')**
Challenging, boulder-like start to the first bolt with the crux soon after. Move right and up to then step across to the wall on the right. Good face climb to the anchors.
Protection: 9 bolts, chain anchors

6. Something About Mary * 5.11b (90')**
Crux at the opening moves and another crux as you exit the hueco further up. The route eases as you move toward the top.
Protection: 10 bolts, chain anchors

Raven Rocks West

Sender One Youth Team on Raven Rocks West. (above and right)

East Canyon Crags 219
Raven Rocks West

Raven Rocks South

East Canyon Crags

Raven Rocks South

Overview
Raven Rocks South is around the corner from the main face and faces into the sun for most of the day. There are six routes ranging from 5.7 -5.11b. The rock quality is great and the belay area is very comfortable.

Approach
From the parking lot at the end of the road, walk up the trail heading east and walk straight to the main face, go right into the belay area for the west crag, but continue on around and to the left to get to the south face.

GPS: 34.664954, -116.977321

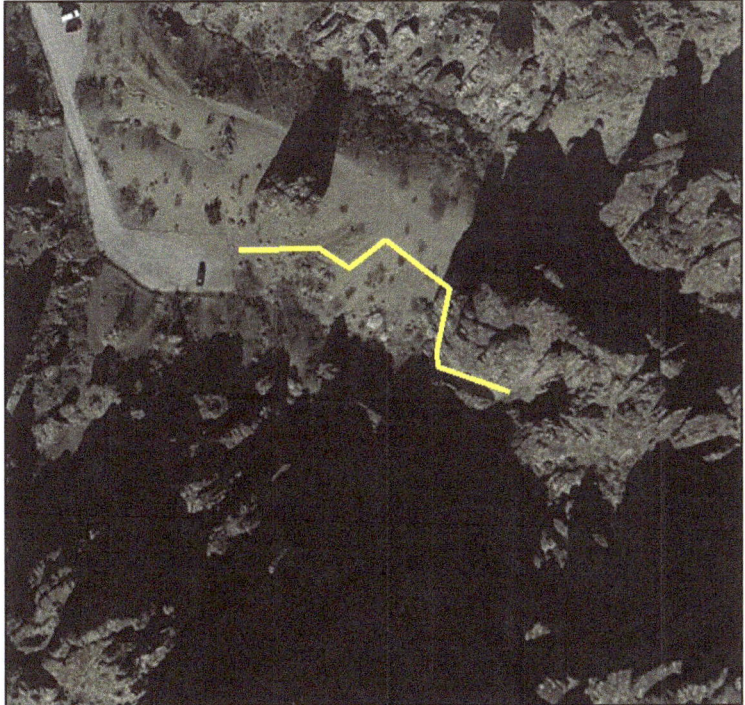

Raven Rocks South

Raven Rocks South

1. Suddenly Susan ** 5.11a (60')
A boulder-like start takes you to the crux just before the second clip. Climb the soft arete to the top. Easier movement as you get higher up. Shares anchors with Taylor Made.
Protection: 8 bolts, chain anchors

2. Taylor Made ** 5.8 (65')
Follow the right arete up easy moves. Shares anchors with Suddenly Susan. A fun lead for the grade. Cruxy start that is remedied with high stepping on slick black rock.
Protection: 8 bolts, chain anchors

Raven Rocks South

Raven Rocks South

1. Custom Tailored ** 5.7 (65')
Easy face climbing with solid holds. A great, long, beginner lead.
Protection: 7 bolts, shut anchors

2. Descending Opinion ** 5.11a (60')
A boulder-like start to easier moves. Stay left of the bolts after the second clip. Take the soft arete to the anchors.
Protection: 7 bolts, shut anchors

3. Candy O * 5.11b (65')**
Face climbing to a crux in the bottom portion. Well-protected route that has a second crux on the last bolt.
Protection: 8 bolts, shut anchors

4. Route 66 * 5.9 (65')**
Sustained climbing that is well-protected. A "New Jack 9". Crux may be at the top for some.
Protection: 7 bolts, chain anchors

Raven Gallery

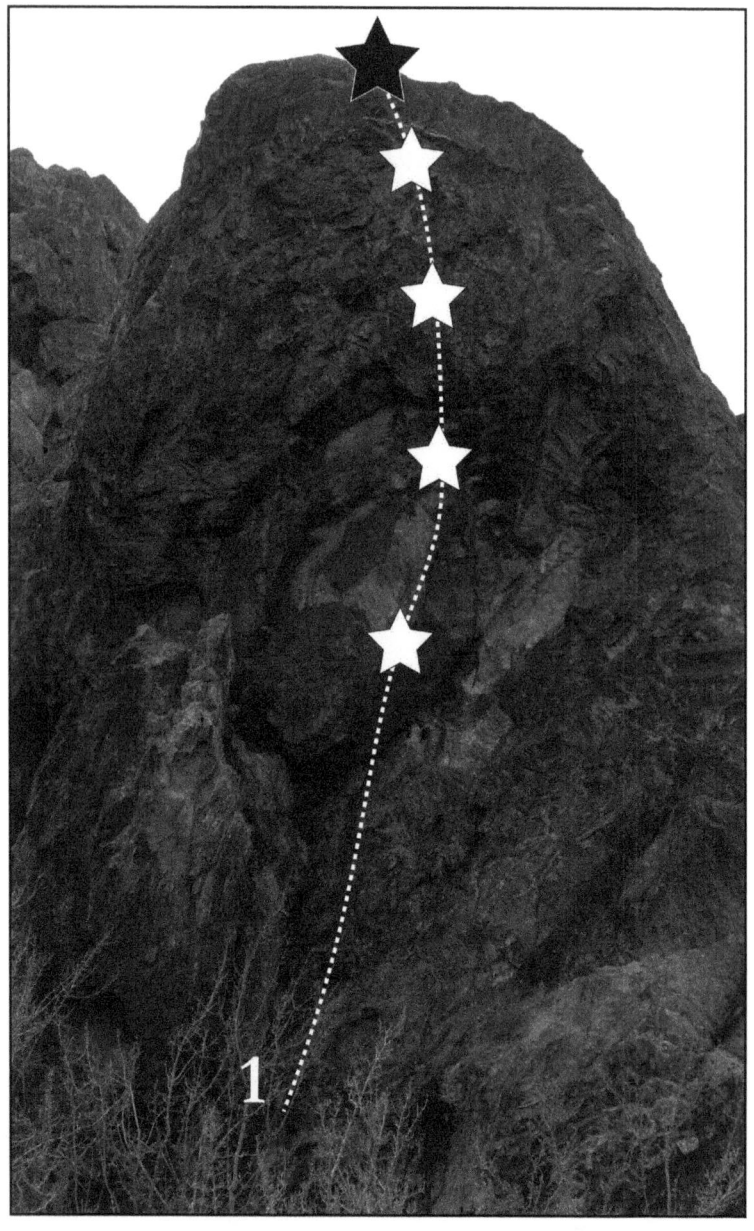

Raven Gallery

Overview
Located in the gully below (southwest of) Raven Rocks West. There are two routes here that were previously undocumented.

1. Mantling 101 5.10b (35')
Protection: 4 bolts, chain anchors

2. Grey Area 5.8 (30')
Protection: 3 bolts, chain anchors

The Getaway

The Getaway

Overview

Located southwest of Raven Rocks, the Getaway is on the hillside facing the parking lot. This crag was never documented and hasn't gotten much traffic. There are some great routes here on excellent rock.

Approach

From the parking lot at the end of the road, walk up the trail heading east and walk straight to the west face of Raven Rocks. Go right into the belay area for the west crag, but continue on around and to the left to get to the south face. Take the trail south down and back up a gully. Scramble up and right, and look for the middle hueco as a guide.

GPS: 34.664497, -116.977673

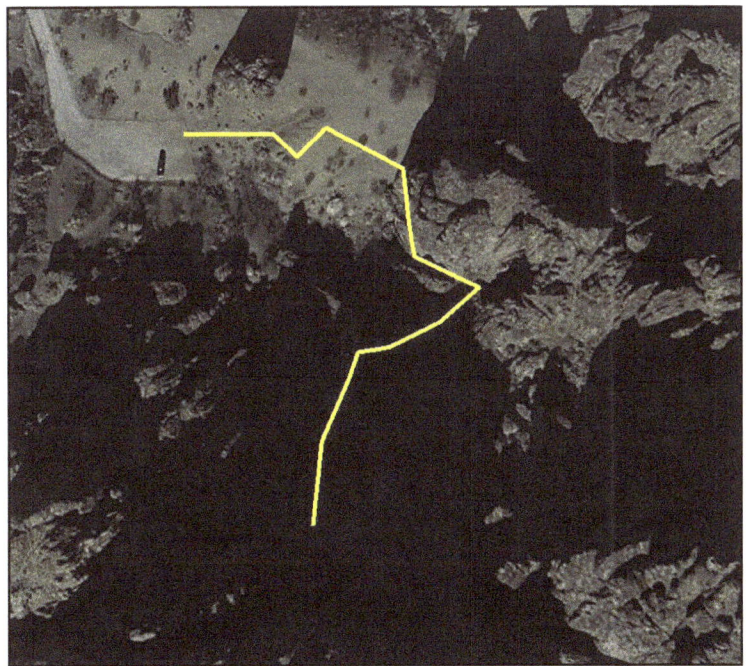

The Getaway

East Canyon Crags 231

The Getaway

The Getaway

East Canyon Crags 233

The Getaway

1. Raleigh World 5.10a (50')
Protection: 4 bolts, chain anchors

2. Getaway *** 5.10a (65')
Protection: 8 bolts, chain anchors

3. Wrangler Arete *** 5.10c (45')
Protection: 4 bolts, chain anchors

4. Smooth as Silk ** 5.11b (60')
Protection: 6 bolts, chain anchors

5. RyBolski ** 5.8 (50')
Protection: 6 bolts, chain anchors

Upper Getaway

Upper Getaway

Overview
The Upper Getaway is a level above The Getaway. It's a steep, 5th class scramble to reach the upper level. There are a few great quality routes with a great view of Raven Rocks.

Approach
Same initial approach as the Getaway. Once there, follow the boulder scramble up to the upper level where Upper Getaway is. Look for the route with the large "shield" on the top.

GPS: 34.664370, -116.977799

1. Stained Glass ** 5.10a (50')
A featured face climb moving left past some vegetation. Continue over the large "shield" at the top.
Protection: 6 bolts, chain anchors

2. Pinhead ** 5.10a (65')
Protection: 5 bolts, shared shut anchors

3. We're A Happy Family * 5.10c (45')(TR)
Protection: top rope, shared shut anchors

Raven's Roost

Overview

Standing alone, south of the Fantasy Island grouping, Raven's Roost has some very underused routes. In the shade most of the year. It can be an OK option on busy days.

1. Kiss 5.10b (50') (5 bolts, shared chain anchors)
2. Snafu 5.8 (50') (5 bolts, shared chain anchors)
3. Step Right Up 5.8 (50') (5 bolts, shared chain anchors)
4. Dead man Walking 5.10a (50') (5 bolts, shared chain anchors)

The Shreen

Overview

From Raven Rocks South, follow the marked trail to the right and up the gully. There is a flat belay area in a small gully just up the trail. Shaded year round.

1. Shreen ** 5.10b (80') (8 bolts, shared chain anchors)
2. Story of J ** 5.10a (80') (8 bolts, shared chain anchors)

Nose Wall

Overview
Located in the valley behind (south of) the Shreen/Fantasy/Fairway. Go to the right of Raven's Roost and scramble up a wash to the very tall crag that looks like the nose of El Capitan at the top.

1. Broken Nose 5.11b (80')
Protection: 8 bolts, chain anchors

Fantasy Island

Overview

Located southeast of Raven Rocks South, Fantasy Island is host to five routes ranging in difficulty from 5.10b-5.11d. It is shaded all day. Rock quality is good.

Approach

Same initial approach as the Shreen. Scramble up loose dirt/rocks farther up the gully then onto the belay ledge in front of the main wall.

GPS: 34.664511, -116.976759

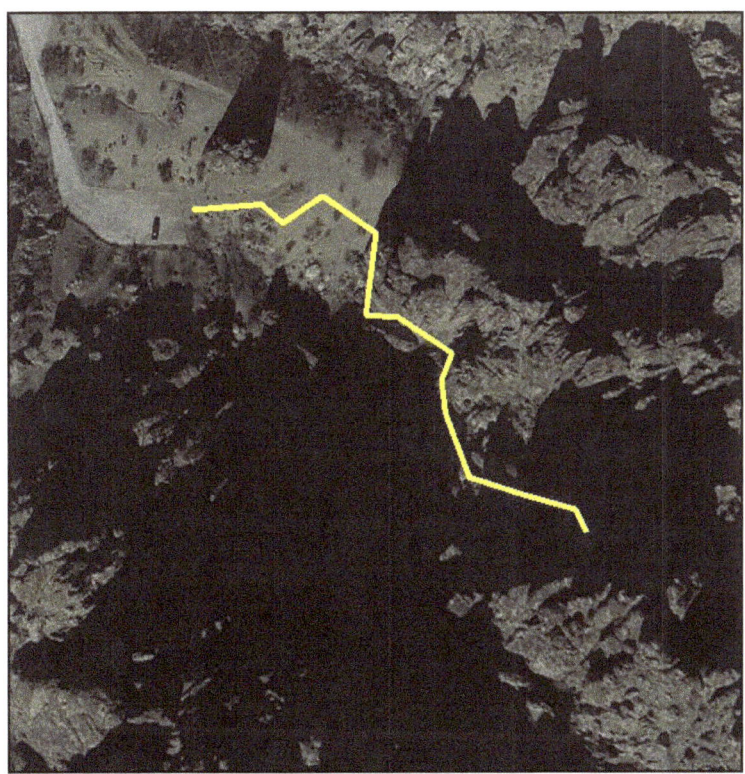

Fantasy Island

1. Vortex 5.11c (35')
2. Flame Thrower 5.11c (75')

Fantasy Island

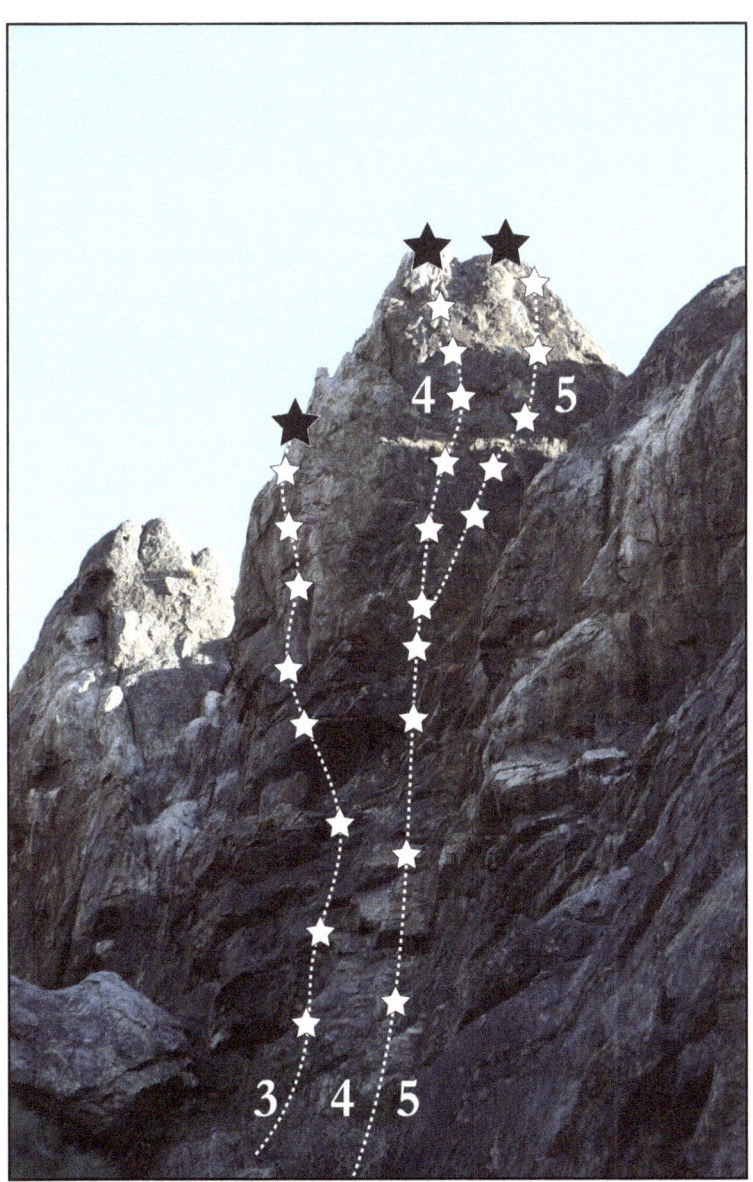

3. Minutemen Arete 5.11d (80')
4. Fantasia 5.11a (95')
5. Mr. Toad's Wild Ride 5.10c (110')

Fantasy Island

1. Vortex ** 5.11c (35')
On the backside of the main face. Start to the right of the recessed triangle and continue up and over it to the left for the crux.
Protection: 5 bolts, chain anchors

2. Flame Thrower ** 5.11c (75')
Starts up on the ledge above Minutemen Arete. Start with the slab and make your way onto the main face. Shares anchors with Minutemen Arete.
Protection: 8 bolts, shut anchors

3. Minutemen Arete **** 5.11d (80')
Start on the slab below Flame Thrower and go up a sustained climb along the arete. Shares anchors with Flame Thrower.
Protection: 8 bolts, chain anchors

4. Fantasia **** 5.11a (95')
Slab start to increasing steepness. Holds get smaller the higher up you go. Excellent route for the grade. Great rock quality.
Protection: 10 bolts, chain anchors

5. Mr. Toad's Wild Ride ** 5.10c (110')
Start with the first 6 bolts of Fantasia until the line breaks off right to finish on separate anchors. Slightly easier and a little longer than Fantasia.
Protection: 10 bolts, chain anchors

The Fairway

Overview
Located south of Raven Rocks, the Fairway is higher up the gully just past Fantasy Island. The Fairway has 12 routes ranging from 5.9-5.12a. It's shady most of the day in the summer and all day in the winter. The rock quality is good, but the approach is steep with a lot of loose rock and dirt.

Approach
Same inital approach as Fantasy Island. At this point there is no discernible trail, so take the path of least resistance. The gully starts to get really loose and steep here. Just past Fantasy Island.

GPS: 34.664011, -116.977013

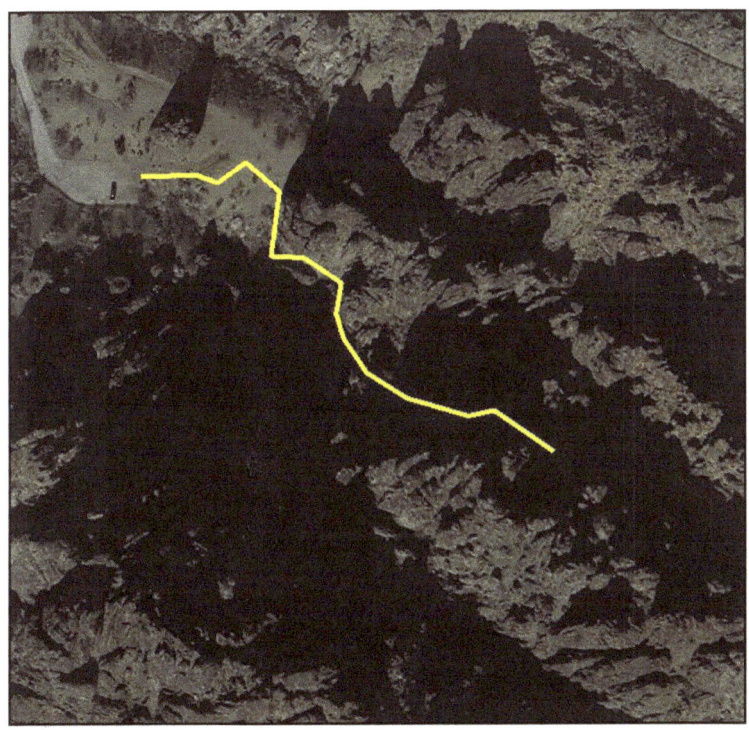

The Fairway

East Canyon Crags

The Fairway

1. Nickel Slots ** 5.11c (50')
Slab start then move right over the "nickel slots" onto easier face climbing to the anchors.
Protection: 5 bolts, chain anchors

2. Mojo Nation * 5.10b (80')(out of view)**
Around the corner of Chaps My Hide. Starts to the right of the chimney and climbs flakes and edges to a long face climb to reach the anchors.
Protection: 8 bolts, shut anchors

3. Chaps My Hide ** 5.11c (80')
Boulder-like start over a hueco onto a large, flaky arete. Easier toward the finish.
Protection: 9 bolts, chain anchors

4. Third Input * 5.12a (90')
Starts on the smooth side of the flake with tricky moves to the ledge joining Mojo Nation for the finish.
Protection: 10 bolts, chain anchors

5. Hole In One * 5.11a (95')**
Climb 3 bolts then take the far left bolt line to the top.
Protection: 10 bolts, chain anchors

6. Shall Remain Nameless ** 5.11c (70')
Climb 3 bolts then take the middle bolt line to the top.
Protection: 8 bolts, chain anchors

7. Face to Face ** 5.11d (70')**
Climb 3 bolts then take the far right bolt line to the top.
Protection: 8 bolts, shut anchors

8. Creepy Hollow ** 5.11b (80')
Creepy looking with challenging moves and a variety of holds.
Protection: 7 bolts, shut anchors

9. My China Girl ** 5.9 (50')
Fun, well-protected route with good exposure.
Protection: 6 bolts, shut anchors

The Fairway

The Fairway

1. Problematic ** 5.10b (70')
Not the best quality compared to the other routes on The Fairway.
Protection: 6 bolts, shut anchors

2. Sky's the Limit ** 5.10b (100')
Start at the base of the bowl and climb up and onto the easy face to the top. This route has cleaned up well over the years.
Protection: 9 bolts, shut anchors

1. Freakshow **** 5.12a (90')
Boulder-like start leads to pumpy and tricky moves to the top.
Protection: 10 fixed chain draws, chain draw anchor

Hard Rock Cafe

Hard Rock Cafe

Overview
Located south of Twin Towers approach trail. Mostly shaded year round.

Approach
From the parking lot at the end of the road, take the trail leading west from the parking lot entrance. Take the south fork up to Hard Rock Cafe. The rocks at the base have a lot of white markings on them.

GPS: 34.664743, -116.978467

1. Between a Rock and a Hard Place * 5.12a/b (60')**
Protection: 7 bolts, shut anchors

2. Potty Training * 5.7 (60')**
Slabby face climb. Fun route that stands by itself on the main wall.
Protection: 5 bolts, Fixe Ring anchors

Slab City

East Canyon Crags

Slab City

Overview
Located directly behind Hard Rock Cafe.

Approach
From the parking lot at the end of the road, take the trail leading west from the parking lot entrance. Take the south fork up to Hard Rock Cafe and go left and behind it. Slab City is "up a level" and behind Hard Rock Cafe.

GPS: 34.664661, -116.978426

1. Brandts Booty ** 5.8- (60')
Left bolt line with positive edges.
Protection: 5 bolts, shared ring anchors

2. D&D ** 5.7 (60')
Right bolt line.
Protection: 6 bolts, shared ring anchors

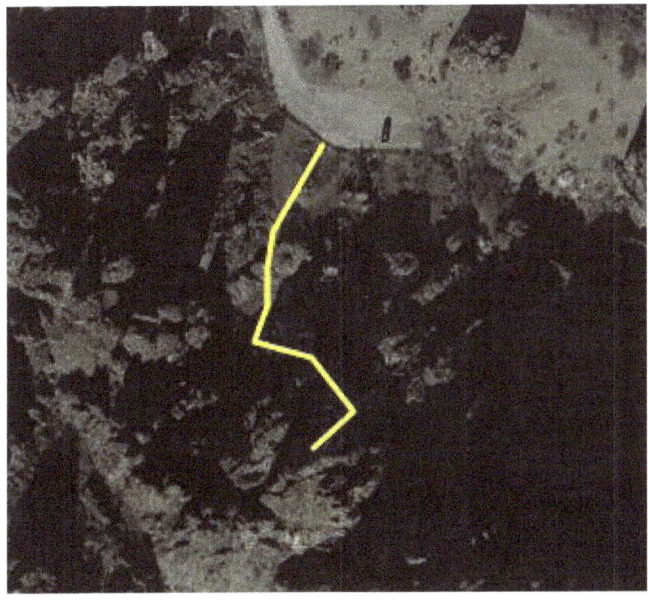

The Finger

The Finger

Overview
Located above and slightly south of Twin Towers. A fun, exposed moderate route.

Approach
From the parking lot at the end of the road, take the trail leading west from the parking lot entrance. Take the well worn trail, zig-zagging up until a steep 4th class spot (its easy up, harder down). At the south face of Twin Towers, follow the trail up and left to a long switchback that puts you on the "balcony" above Twin Towers.

GPS: 34.664627, -116.978696

1. Crooked Dick Spire * 5.9 (35')**
Boulder-like start to the crux between the 2nd and 3rd bolt.
Protection: 4 bolts, chain anchors

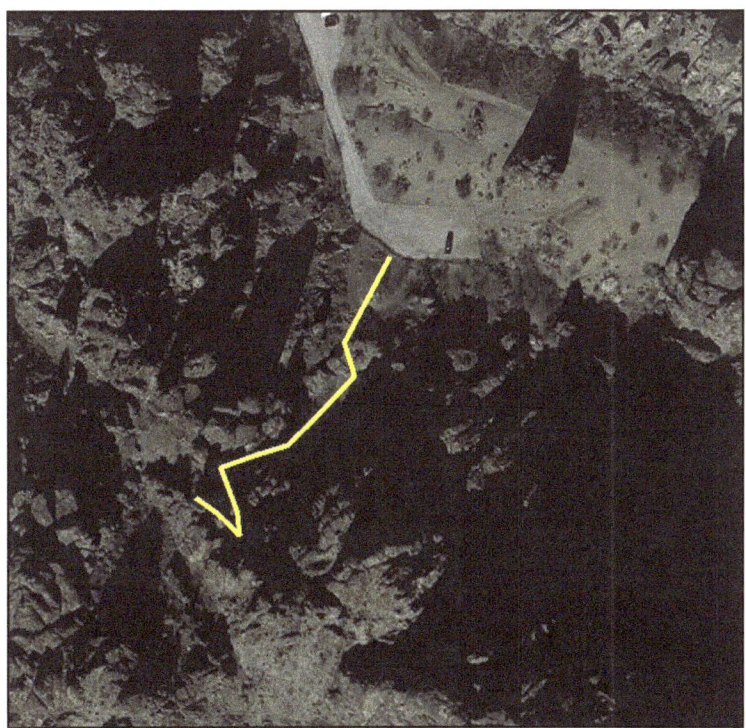

Prodigy Pile

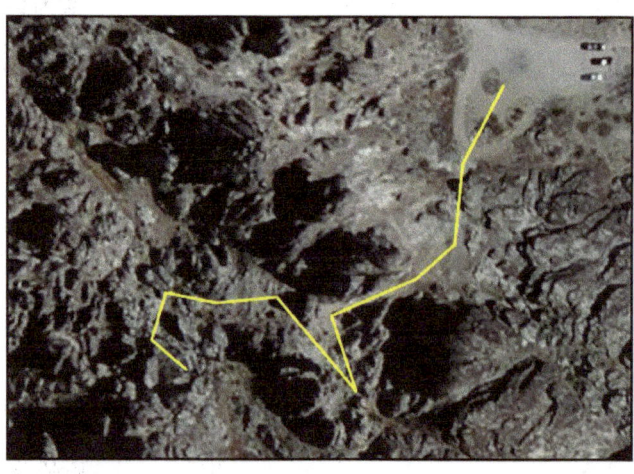

Prodigy Pile

Overview
Located directly west and in the small canyon behind Crooked Dick Spire. Developed by Louie Anderson. He, Chris Lindner, and Daniel Woods are the only known ascents.

Approach
From the parking lot at the end of the road, take the trail leading west from the parking lot entrance. Take the well worn trail zig zagging up until a tricky 4th class spot (it's easy up, hard down). At the south face of Twin Towers, follow the trail up and left to a long switchback that puts you on the "balcony" above Twin Towers. Scramble down into the small canyon and go around the large boulder in the middle to reach Prodigy Pile.

GPS: 34.664578, -116.979216

1. Fire Starter *** 5.13d (25')
Small crimps up a steep face.
Protection: 5 bolts, shut anchors

Twin Towers

Twin Towers

Overview
Located on the ridge and south of Pat and Jack Pinnacle. Below and to the right of Crooked Dick Spire. It's sunny at most times of the day. There are 12 routes ranging from 5.8-5.12b.

Approach
From the parking lot at the end of the road, take the trail leading west from the parking lot entrance. Take the well-worn trail, zig-zagging up until a tricky 4th class spot (it's easy up, hard down) to reach the belay notch for Twin Towers.

GPS: 34.664670, -116.978751

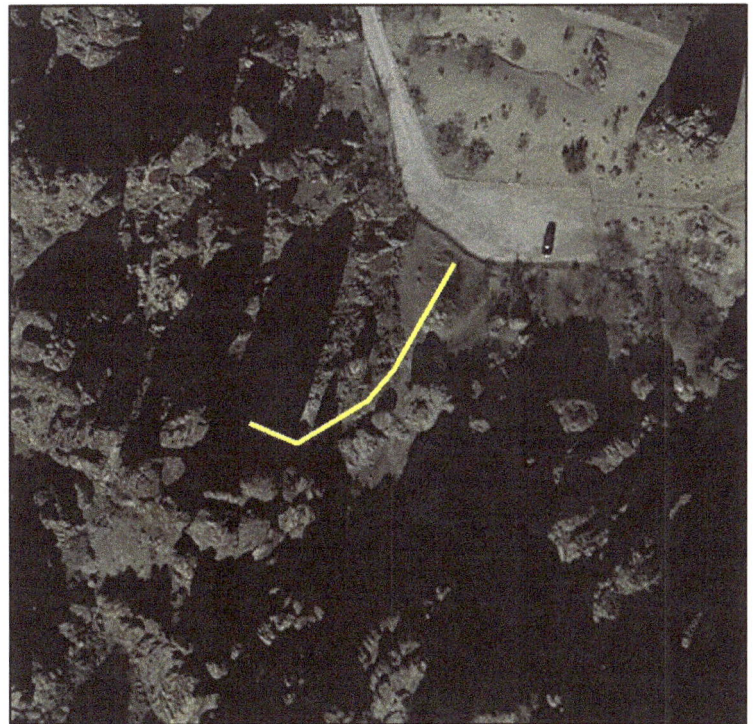

Twin Towers - South Face

Twin Towers - South Face

1. Soft Core ** 5.8 (45')
Fun, sustained route with no standout crux.
Protection: 6 bolts, shut anchors

2. Fine Day ** 5.10a (45')
Well-protected, moderate route. Small roof crux at the 2nd bolt.
Protection: 6 bolts, shut anchors

3. Sort of Silly * 5.10a (45')
Technical moves until you reach the crack. Climb the right side of the crack up an easier face. Shares anchors with Lock Down.
Protection: 6 bolts, shared shut anchors

4. Lock Down ** 5.10c (45')
Boulder-like start to a high first bolt. Climb left of the middle of the tower and join Sort of Silly for the last two bolts. Shared anchor with Sort of Silly.
Protection: 6 bolts, shared shut anchors

5. Carnival In Hell *** 5.11d (45')
Well-protected and right up the middle of the right tower. Shares anchors with Nightstick. Very hard for the grade.
Protection: 6 bolts, shared chain anchors

6. Nightstick ** 5.11a (50')
Another well-protected face climb with a crux in the middle. Shares anchors with Carnival In Hell.
Protection: 6 bolts, shared chain anchors

Twin Towers - East Face

Twin Towers - East Face

1. Concrete Blonde ** 5.11c (75')
Crux traverse in the beginning. Start in the corner.
Protection: 9 bolts, chain anchors

2. Date with Destiny *** 5.12d (75')
Face climb to get to the roof crux. Long face climb to reach the anchors.
Protection: 2 bolts, 3 chain draws, 2 more bolts, chain anchors

3. Funny Like A Funeral *** 5.12a (75')
Start in the notch and climb up the crack. Take the steep wall up to a long face climb.
Protection: 8 bolts, chain anchors

4. No Billy No 5.12a (75')
Balancy face climb all the way to the top. Start opposite the Funny Like a Funeral notch.
Protection: 7 bolts, chain anchors

5. Macho Insecurity 5.11a (35') (next page)
Protection: 4 bolts, chain anchors

6. Tight Black Vinyl 5.11a (50') (not pictured)
Past Macho Insecurity and up at the top of the gully on the north side.
Protection: 6 Bolts, shut anchors

Twin Towers - North Face

East Canyon Crags **263**

Pat and Jack Pinnacle

Overview
Located on the ridge between Twin Towers and Lethal Rock. Afternoon shade and an easy approach. There are four routes ranging from 5.10a -5.12a.

Approach
From the parking lot at the end of the road, take the trail leading west from the parking lot entrance. Take the trail directly up the hill, heading to the right of Twin Towers. Pat and Jack Pinnacle has the long "Wave" at its base.

GPS: 34.664892, -116.978796

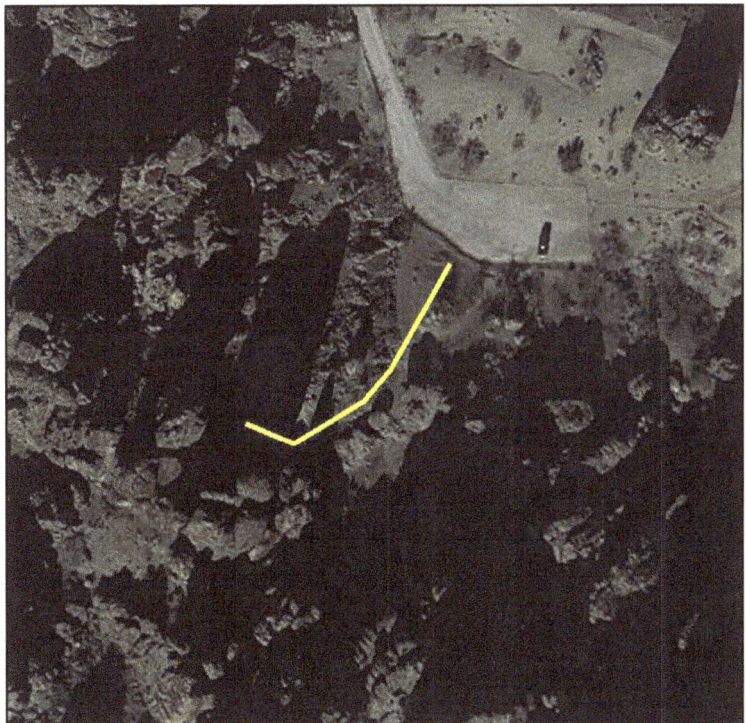

Pat and Jack Pinnacle

Pat and Jack Pinnacle

1. Campbell Soup * 5.10a (50')
Protection: 6 bolts, chain anchors

2. Pat and Jack ** 5.11b (50')
Protection: 6 bolts, chain anchors

3. Fair Weather Friend ** 5.11d (50')
Protection: 6 bolts, chain anchors

4. Patty Cake ** 5.12a (75')
Protection: 7 bolts, chain anchors

Lethal Rock

Lethal Rock

Overview

Located on the ridge to the north of Pat and Jack Pinnacle. It's slightly south and behind Crossfire Crag. Lethal Rock is a challenging, steep, and pumpy wall. Routes range in difficulty from 5.9 to 5.13b. It's mostly sunny all day.

Approach

From the parking lot at the end of the road, take the trail leading west from the parking lot entrance. Take the trail directly up the hill heading to the right of Twin Towers. Walk past Pat and Jack Pinnacle and veer up the hill and head west.

GPS: 34.664985, -116.978975

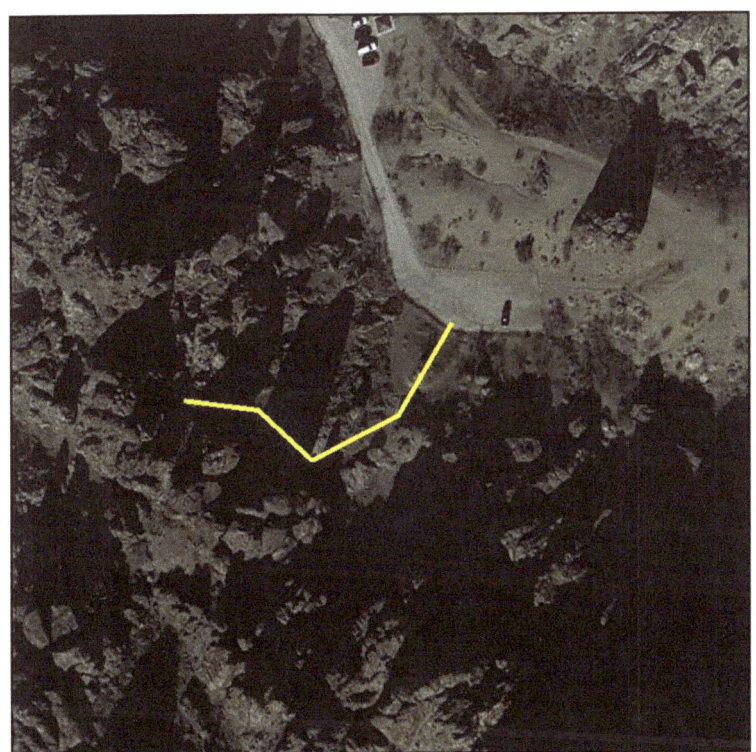

Lethal Rock

East Canyon Crags

Lethal Rock

1. Marked for Death * 5.11b (50')
Stay left of the arete. Keep your balance to fend off the pump.
Protection: 6 bolts, shut anchors

2. Lethal Weapon * 5.12d (50')**
A classic, steep route with sustained difficulty and variety of moves.
Protection: 1 bolt and 4 chain draws, chain anchors

3. Death Wish * 5.12d (50')**
A reachy climb up the steep face. Sustained difficulty.
Protection: 6 bolts, clip in anchors

4. Under the Gun * 5.13b (75')**
One of the hardest routes in the canyon.
Protection: 6 bolts, chain anchors

5. Chick Route * 5.9 (65')
Start below and climb toward the ledge. Start the second level onto the top. This is located right of the face.
Protection: 6 bolts, chain anchors

The Fin

East Canyon Crags **271**

The Fin

Overview
Located directly west of the parking lot entrance. A 2-minute walk up a slow hill. Just south of Crossfire Crag.

Approach
From the main parking lot, walk west toward Crossfire Crag and then just south to the big fin. It's about a 2-minute walk.

GPS: 34.665294, -116.978617

1. Maynard G. Krebs * 5.12b (30')**
Protection: 5 bolts , chain anchors

2. Guttermouth * 5.11d (30')
Protection: 3 bolts, shut anchors

3. Shooting Spree ** 5.11c (60')
Protection: 6 bolts, shut anchors

4. Friendly Fire ** 5.11c (60')
Protection: 6 bolts, chain anchors

Crossfire Crag

East Canyon Crags

Crossfire Crag

Overview
Crossfire Crag is the large wall that looks east over the parking lot. Great selection of routes on excellent rock with virtually no approach. Difficulty ranges from 5.9- 5.13b. Morning sun and afternoon shade.

Approach
From the main parking lot, walk west, meandering through small boulders to arrive at the base. It's about a 2-minute walk.

GPS: 34.665350, -116.978550

Crossfire Crag

East Canyon Crags

Crossfire Crag

Crossfire Crag

Crossfire Crag

1. Jug Haul ** 5.9 (40')
Protection: 5 bolts , shut anchors

2. Improbable ** 5.11a (55')
Protection: 6 bolts, shut anchors

3. The Possibility * 5.11d (70')**
Protection: 9 bolts, chain anchors

4. Evil Offspring * 5.12c (65')**
Protection: 8 bolts, chain anchors

5. Bad Seed ** 5.13b (50')
Protection: 5 bolts , chain anchors

6. Double Kneebar Ranch ** 5.12b (50')**
Protection: 4 bolts, shut anchors

7. Crossfire * 5.12a (80')**
Protection: 9 bolts, chain anchors

8. Split the Scene * 5.12b (90')
Protection: 10 bolts , chain anchors

9. The Scene Is Not For Sale * 5.11a (90')**
Protection: 10 bolts, chain anchors

10. Change of Scene * 5.10a (90')**
Protection: 10 bolts, shut anchors

50' right of Change of Scene on a separate wall (next page)
11. The Last Coyote * 5.12+ (50')**
Protection: 5 bolts, shut anchors

20' right of Last Coyote on a separate crag (next page)
12. Short and Sassy ** 5.11b (50')
Protection: 5 bolts, chain anchors

Crossfire Crag

East Canyon Crags

Crossfire Crag

Boy Scout Wall

Boy Scout Wall

Overview
Boy Scout Wall is a moderate-grade playground. With 19 routes ranging from 5.5-5.10d, this wall can be pretty crowded. The only group campsite is adjacent, so be aware that this is a prime spot to be taken over by groups on the weekend. Its in the shade all day, year round. The rock quality is superb with features galore.

Approach
It's just south of the big group campsite and the last large parking area before Parking Lot Rock (visible on the east side of the road, farther south). There are four picnic tables under a large ramada. There is parking right in front of the wall. Walk about 60' from the parking area and scramble over a 4-foot boulder to take the well-established trail up and to the west end of the Boy Scout Wall. You can also follow the road and cut in to the crag to reach the south section

GPS: 34.666275, -116.979505

Boy Scout Wall

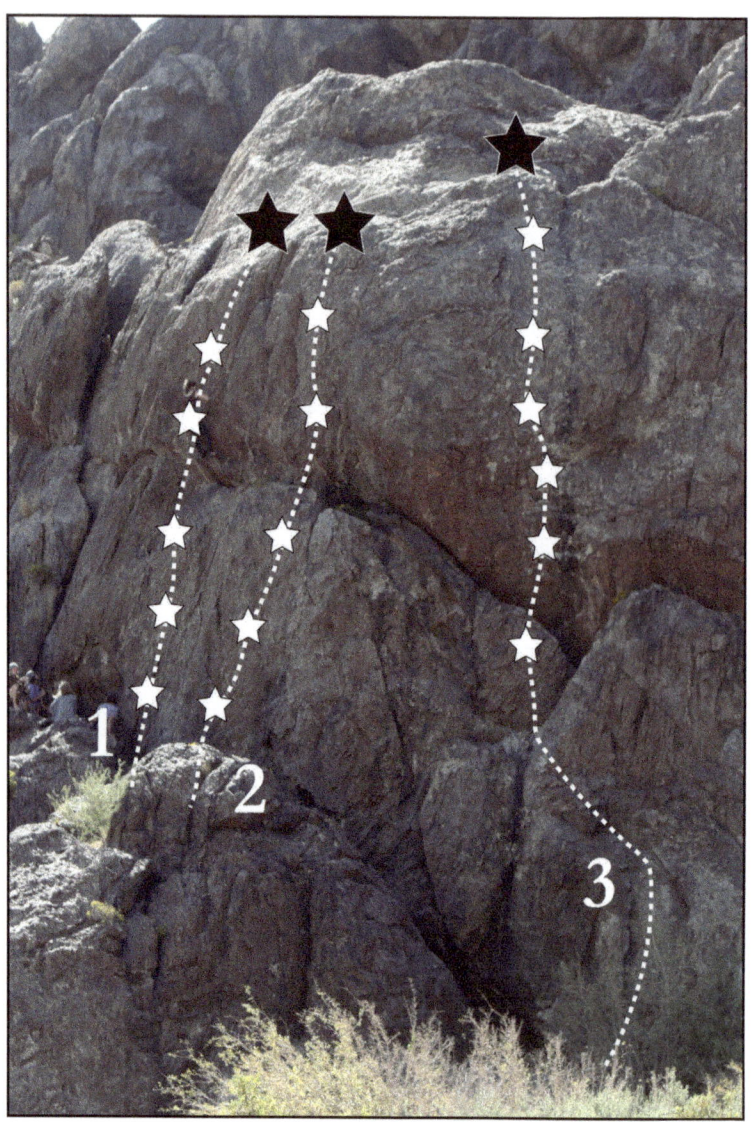

1. Pussy Pie 5.9 (40')
2. Venus Envy 5.10a (40')
3. Dog Ate the Homework 5.10a (65')

Boy Scout Wall

4. Left Flank 5.10a (85')
5. Midway 5.10d (85')
6. Make a Way 5.10b (80')
7. Three Giant Steps 5.10a (85')
8. Reaching Rayane 5.9 (70')

Boy Scout Wall

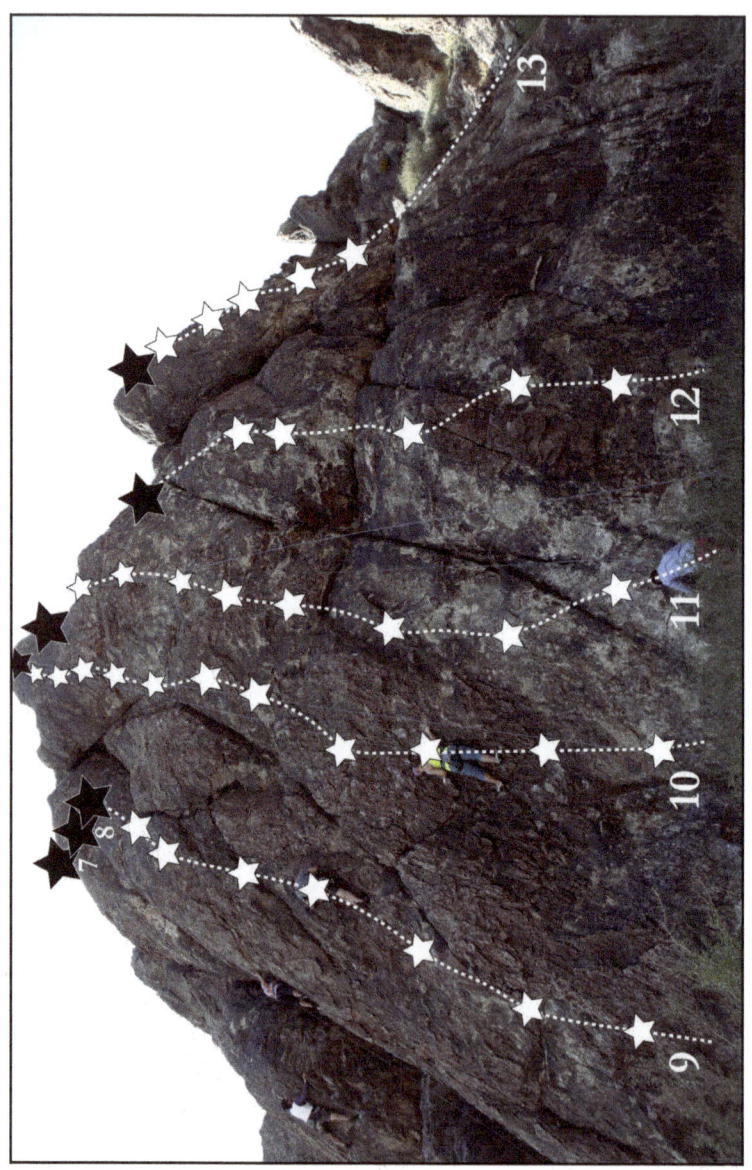

Boy Scout Wall

Topo Left
9. Cool Enough 5.8 (70')
10. Jack Be Nimble 5.9 (75')
11. Sam I Am 5.8 (70')
12. Green Eggs and Ham 5.7 (50')
13. Girl Scout Cookies 5.7 (50')

Topo Above
14. Unleash the Dragon 5.8 (40')
15. Ivy Alice 5.6 (35')
16. Truculence 5.6 (40')

Boy Scout Wall

17. Blitzo's Pile 5.5 (25')
18. Ashbug 5.10a (45')(TR)
19. Overkill 5.11c (65')

Boy Scout Wall

1. Pussy Pie ** 5.9 (40')
Far left route on the first section of Boy Scout Wall. Scramble to ledge.
Protection: 5 bolts, ring anchors

2. Venus Envy ** 5.10a (40')
Slightly harder version of Pussy Pie.
Protection: 5 bolts, ring anchors

3. Dog Ate the Homework ** 5.10a (65')
Starts at the base of the wall. Anchors farther back from the top.
Protection: 6 bolts, ring anchors

4. Left Flank ** 5.10a (85')
Climb past the overhang to a sustained climb to a bulge before the top.
Protection: 6 bolts, shared chain anchors

5. Midway * 5.10d (85')**
Boulder-like hueco crux to start. Sustained and easier to the top.
Protection: 7 bolts, shared chain anchors

6. Make A Way * 5.10b (80')**
Protection: 7 bolts, shared chain anchors

7. Three Giant Steps * 5.10a (85')**
Protection: 9 bolts, chain anchors

8. Reaching Rayane * 5.9 (70')**
Start up the face, just left of the crevice. Sustained difficulty and fun moves to the top.
Protection: 7 bolts, chain anchors

9. Cool Enough ** 5.8 (70')
Fun, easy lead. Crux is at the start.
Protection: 7 bolts, shut anchors

10. Jack be Nimble * 5.9 (75')**
Start right of the seam. Fun, well-protected climb. Orphan bolt on right. Move left around the top face to reach out for the anchors (to your right).
Protection: 11 bolts, shut anchors

Boy Scout Wall

11. Sam I Am * 5.8 (70')**
Feature-filled climb that passes the right side of the big scoop.
Protection: 8 bolts, shut anchors

12. Green Eggs and Ham ** 5.7 (50')
Hard for the grade, but a fun climb. Crux at the 4th bolt.
Protection: 5 bolts, ring anchor

13. Girl Scout Cookies ** 5.7 (50')
Unprotected, big slab start (20' or so, but 4th class). North-facing wall before the west-facing corridor.
Protection: 5 bolts, ring anchors

14. Unleash the Dragon ** 5.8 (40')
Fun face climb with lots of features. Shares a fourth bolt and anchor with Ivy Alice.
Protection: 4 bolts, ring anchors

15. Ivy Alice ** 5.6 (35')
Fun climb with lots of jugs and great footholds. Shares the fourth bolt and anchor with Unleash the Dragon. Starts left of the boulder.
Protection: 4 bolts, ring anchors

16. Truculence ** 5.6 (40')
Start to the right of the big boulder to the first bolt. Move left and continue toward the anchors
Protection: 5 bolts, chain anchors

17. Blitzo's Pile ** 5.5 (25')
Short and fun route, back where the corridor starts to narrow.
Protection: 3 bolts, chain anchors

18. Ashbug ** 5.10a (45') (Top Rope)
Back in the corridor across from backside of Boy Scout Wall.
Protection: Top rope anchors

19. Overkill * 5.11c (65')**
Farther Back in the corridor across from backside of Boy Scout Wall.
Protection: 7 Bolts, ring anchors

Routes by Grade

5.5

Blitzo's Pile ** 5.5, 288

5.6

Ivy Alice ** 5.6, 288
Little Jack Horner * 5.6, 175
N00b Slab 5.6, 59
Something borrowed something n00b 5.6, 110
Truculence ** 5.6, 288
Whiter Shade of Pale ** 5.6, 55

5.7

Cheap Lipstick ** 5.7, 182
Custom Tailored ** 5.7, 225
D&D ** 5.7, 251
Girl Scout Cookies ** 5.7, 288
Green Eggs and Ham ** 5.7, 288
It Puts the Lotion on its Skin 5.7, 148
Kestrel Dihedral 5.7, 149
Korean Wall Route 1 5.7, 145
My Side of the Roadside ** 5.7, 63
n00b Arete 5.7, 110
Potty Training *** 5.7, 249
Powder Puff ** 5.7, 182
Rattle the Cattle * 5.7, 197
Uncle Funs Basement *** 5.7, 154
White Flight * 5.7, 55

5.8

Barney ** 5.8, 75
Beyond the Crucified ** 5.8, 197
Brandts Booty ** 5.8-, 251
Cool Enough ** 5.8, 287
Cupid's Fever *** 5.8, 49
Grey Area 5.8, 227
Hale Bop Tango ** 5.8, 197
Inconceivable *** 5.8, 154
Mostly Dead ** 5.8, 154
Redneck ** 5.8, 139

5.8 Cont.

RyBolski ** 5.8, 233
Sam I Am *** 5.8, 288
Snafu 5.8, 236
Soft Core ** 5.8, 259
Step Right Up 5.8, 236
Taylor Made ** 5.8, 223
Toe Tag ** 5.8, 158
Unleash the Dragon ** 5.8, 288
Victoria's Secret *** 5.8, 49
Walk in the Park * 5.8, 182

5.9

Bombs Away 5.9, 148
Brandts Booty ** -5.8, 251
Central High 5.9, 128
Chick Route * 5.9, 269
Crooked Dick Spire *** 5.9, 253
Destination Oblivion 5.9, 154
Dita's Play House 5.9+, 148
Dry Spell ** 5.9, 57
Easy Prey ** 5.9, 128
Fred *** 5.9, 75
Fun in the Sun ** 5.9, 182
Hidden Grotto Left 5.9, 152
Indirect Action *** 5.9, 199
Jack be Nimble *** 5.9, 287
Jug Haul ** 5.9, 277
La Fissura 5.9, 191
My China Girl ** 5.9, 245
Pussy Pie ** 5.9, 287
Reaching Rayane *** 5.9, 287
Roadside Warrior *** 5.9, 63
Rob's Rambunctious Ride ** 5.9, 217
Route 66 *** 5.9, 225
Sunny Up ** 5.9, 115
The Crawl Space ** 5.9, 158
White Head ** 5.9, 55
Woody 5.9, 142
Working Men R Pissed 5.9, 199
72 Hour Hold 5.9, 199

Routes by Grade

5.10a

Ashbug ** 5.10a, 288
Balancing Act 5.10a, 204
Campbell Soup * 5.10a, 265
Change of Scene *** 5.10a, 277
City Slicker ** 5.10a, 139
Cosgrove Tower 5.10+, 151
Dead man Walking 5.10a, 236
Decaf ** 5.10a, 209
Dog Ate the Homework ** 5.10a, 287
Fine Day ** 5.10a, 259
Getaway *** 5.10a, 233
Goldfinger * 5.10a, 182
Holy Moley *** 5.10a, 211
Idiots At Happy Hour *** 5.10a, 92
Left Flank ** 5.10a, 287
Little Red Book *** 5.10a, 204
My Bloody Valentine *** 5.10a, 49
Pinhead ** 5.10a, 235
Raleigh World 5.10a, 233
Red Headed She Devil 5.10+, 154
Ryane's Revenge ** 5.10a, 188
Sophie's Choice * 5.10a, 190
Sort of Silly * 5.10a, 259
Stained Glass ** 5.10a, 235
Step Across *** 5.10a, 217
Story of J ** 5.10a, 237
Sunshine Superman * 5.10a, 115
Technically Inept *** 5.10a, 97
The Flake ** 5.10a, 139
Three Giant Steps *** 5.10a, 287
Venus Envy ** 5.10a, 287
Welcome to New Jack City *** 5.10a, 217
What The...* 5.10a, 191
You Just Got Jacked 5.10a, 57

5.10b

Another Piece of Meat 5.10b, 196
Buzz 5.10b, 142
Celebate Rifle ** 5.10b, 137
Crew of One 5.10b, 133
Dr. Know ** 5.10b, 182

5.10b Cont.

Generous Portions ** 5.10b, 57
Hidden Grotto Right 5.10a/b, 152
Kiss 5.10b, 236
Make A Way *** 5.10b, 287
Mantling 101 5.10b, 227
Mojo Nation *** 5.10b, 245
Poaching Bighorns *** 5.10b, 79
Problematic ** 5.10b, 247
RepoMan * 5.10b, 211
Shreen ** 5.10b, 237
Sky's the Limit ** 5.10b, 247
The Roundup ** 5.10b, 137
White Out *** 5.10b, 55

5.10c

Bitter End *** 5.10c, 188
Black Jack 5.10b/c, 99
Catalina **** 5.10c, 79
Chick Flaky *** 5.10c, 182
Espresso *** 5.10c, 209
Gallows Pole 5.10c, 89
Gonna Be Just Like Them ** 5.10c, 85
Good day Sunshine *** 5.10c, 115
Korean Wall Route 2 5.10c, 145
Lock Down ** 5.10c, 259
Love Onsite*** 5.10c, 217
Mr. Toad's Wild Ride ** 5.10c, 242
One Eyed Jack ** 5.10c, 133
Red Tape 5.10c, 97
Same Same but Different ** 5.10c, 217
Should be Called Do What? ** 5.10c, 211
Sundowner 5.10c, 196
Tough Choices ** 5.10c, 213
We're A Happy Family * 5.10c, 235
What's New Jack *** 5.10c, 115
Wrangler Arete *** 5.10c, 233

5.10d

All I Can Grab *** 5.10d, 81
Camp Stalker ** 5.10d, 133
Curly * 5.10d, 139
Demolition Man 5.10d, 196
From the Ashes 5.10d, 196
Midway *** 5.10d, 287
Room for Improvement *** 5.10d, 188
Shaky Start 5.10d, 204
Snow White *** 5.10d, 55
The Snake *** 5.10d, 81
Unknown Route 5.10d, 204

5.11a

1964 5.11+, 150
2016 5.11+, 150
Blast from the Past ** 5.11a, 211
California Dreamin * 5.11a, 34
Dance This ** 5.11a, 188
Descending Opinion ** 5.11a, 225
Drunken Midget Wrestling 5.11a, 87
Fantasia **** 5.11a, 242
Funny Face *** 5.11a, 139
Getty-Up ** 5.11a, 137
Gut Reaction 5.11a, 177
Hole In One *** 5.11a, 245
Improbable ** 5.11a, 277
Legion of Evil *** 5.11a, 81
Life Returns 5.11a, 196
Macho Insecurity 5.11a, 261
Nightstick ** 5.11a, 259
Oh Behive 5.11a, 57
Roughneck *** 5.11a, 137
Sluttering ** 5.11a, 188
Stemroids ** 5.11a, 55
Suddenly Susan ** 5.11a, 223
The 4 Horsemen **** 5.11a, 158
The Pups Are Doggin' It 5.11a, 190
The Raven ** 5.11a, 211
The Scene Is Not For Sale *** 5.11a, 277
Tight Black Vinyl 5.11a, 261

5.11a Cont.

Toxic Box ** 5.11a, 81
Use Your Mind *** 5.11a, 57
Vertigo ** 5.11a, 126
Violent Arrest 5.11+, 90
Voyeur ** 5.11a, 139
Watchtower Direct * 5.11a, 156
Will Power ** 5.11a, 213

5.11b

Ape Index 5.11b, 45
Black Widow ** 5.11b, 133
Bonus Fat ** 5.11b, 128
Broken Nose 5.11b, 238
Bumper Brigade 5.11a/b, 44
Candy O *** 5.11b, 225
Creepy Hollow ** 5.11b, 245
Crucified 5.11b, 196
Good to be Awake *** 5.11b, 188
Gun for Hire *** 5.11b, 188
Hang Daddy ** 5.11b, 57
Headhunter 5.11b, 39
Hero Worship *** 5.11b, 126
Korean Wall Route 3 5.11b, 145
Marked For Death * 5.11b, 269
One More Victim 5.11b, 196
Pat and Jack ** 5.11b, 265
Propaganda * 5.11b, 65
Sex Dance ** 5.11b, 188
Sex Predator/Deviant *** 5.11b, 126
She Packs Her Bags for Outer Space * 5.11b, 59
Short and Sassy ** 5.11b, 277
Smooth As Silk ** 5.11b, 233
Something About Mary *** 5.11b, 217
Straight Ahead ** 5.11b, 123
This Nazi Shit Won't Do 5.11b, 128
To Infinity and Beyond 5.11b, 142
Waiting For Anarchy *** 5.11b, 92

5.11c

Bog of Eternal Stench 5.11b/c, 158
Chaps My Hide ** 5.11c, 245

5.11c Cont.

Concrete Blonde ** 5.11c, 261
Crowd Pleaser 5.11b/c, 44
Flame Thrower ** 5.11c, 242
Friendly Fire ** 5.11c, 271
Hidden Agenda **** 5.11c, 139
Lady In Red 5.11c, 99
Life of the Party ** 5.11c, 35
Little Stiffy *** 5.11c, 204
Lost Your Edge 5.11c, 141
Nickel Slots ** 5.11c, 245
Overkill *** 5.11c, 288
Shall Remain Nameless ** 5.11c, 245
Shooting Spree ** 5.11c, 271
Stop Staring At My Ass ** 5.11b/c, 97
Tradliness 5.11c, 92
Vortex ** 5.11c, 242

5.11d

Backside Arete *** 5.11d, 177
Been to the Edge 5.11d, 141
Brown Recluse *** 5.11c/d, 133
Carnival In Hell *** 5.11d, 259
Chemical Warfare 5.11d, 85
Cool To Be You 5.11d/12a, 97
Face to Face **** 5.11d, 245
Fair Weather Friend ** 5.11d, 265
Guttermouth * 5.11d, 271
King of all Media *** 5.11d, 177
Minutemen Arete **** 5.11d, 242
Offwidth 5.11d, 139
On the Fringe ** 5.11d, 31
Rainbow Drive *** 5.11d, 123
Six Pack ** 5.11d, 177
The Possibility *** 5.11d, 277
They All Look the Same ** 5.11d, 188
Westward Ho * 5.11d, 59

5.12a

Back from the Dead *** 5.12a, 177
Back with a Bang ** 5.12a, 199
Clumsy*** 5.12a, 65
Cromag *** 5.12a, 137
Crossfire *** 5.12a, 277
Freakshow **** 5.12a, 247
Funny Like A funeral *** 5.12a, 261
Hangman 5.12a, 89
Nervous Breakdown 5.12a, 89
No Billy No 5.12a, 261
Patty Cake ** 5.12a, 265
Red Hot ** 5.12a, 182
Red Tail Arete ** 5.12a, 133
Solitary Confinement *** 5.12a, 124
Stop the Madness *** 5.12a, 204
The Last Coyote *** 5.12+, 277
Third Input * 5.12a, 245
Tommy Thompson Route 5.12a, 39

5.12b

Between a Rock and a Hard Place *** 5.12a/b, 249
Body Scum ** 5.12b, 126
Crack in the Armor *** 5.12b, 126
Double Kneebar Ranch **** 5.12b, 277
Guilt Free ** 5.12b, 65
Guilty as Sin ** 5.12b, 65
Hateful Little Girl 5.12b, 65
Lost in the Middle **** 5.12b, 65
Maynard G. Krebs *** 5.12b, 271
Mental Block ** 5.12b, 126
No Use for a Name ** 5.12b, 109
Power Grab 5.12a/b, 89
Red Devil *** 5.12b, 207
Sniper 5.12a/b, 31
Split the Scene * 5.12b, 277
The Critic 5.12b, 41
Tikiman 5.12b, 39

Routes by Grade

5.12c

Combination Lock ** 5.12c, 126
Deadbolt 5.12c, 39
Disconnected ** 5.12c, 207
Evil Offspring *** 5.12c, 277
Let's Kung Fu ** 5.12c, 177
Madam X 5.12c, 65
Sex Magik ** 5.12c, 126
The Meat 5.12c, 39
The Predator *** 5.12c, 126
Walk the Talk *** 5.12c, 199
You Don't Know Jack **** 5.12c, 207

5.12d

Date With Destiny *** 5.12d, 261
Death Wish *** 5.12d, 269
Hallraker **** 5.12d, 124
Lethal Weapon *** 5.12d, 269
Ride the Wild *** 5.12d, 109
You Get What You Deserve *** 5.12d, 65

5.13a

The Action **** 5.13a, 156
The DX 5.13a, 150
The Travesty **** 5.13a, 109
Voodoo Lounge *** 5.13a, 207

5.13b

Bad Seed ** 5.13b, 277
Master of None **** 5.13b, 35
Under the Gun *** 5.13b, 269
Voodoo Child *** 5.13b, 207

5.13c/d

Fire Starter *** 5.13d, 25
Shell Shock 5.13b/c, 31

Index

A

All I Can Grab *** 5.10d 81
Another Piece of Meat 5.10b 196
Ape Index 5.11b 45
Ashbug ** 5.10a 288

B

Back from the Dead *** 5.12a 177
Backside Arete *** 5.11d 177
Back with a Bang ** 5.12a 199
Bad Seed ** 5.13b 277
Balancing Act 5.10a 204
Barney ** 5.8 75
Been to the Edge 5.11d 141
Between a Rock and a Hard Place *** 5.12a/b 249
Beyond the Crucified ** 5.8 197
Bitter End *** 5.10c 188
Black Jack 5.10b/c 99
Black Widow ** 5.11b 133
Blast from the Past ** 5.11a 211
Blitzo's Pile ** 5.5 288
Body Scum ** 5.12b 126
Bog of Eternal Stench 5.11b/c 158
Bombs Away 5.9 148
Bonus Fat ** 5.11b 128
Brandts Booty ** 5.8- 251
Broken Nose 5.11b 238
Brown Recluse *** 5.11c/d 133
Bumper Brigade 5.11a/b 44
Buzz 5.10b 143

C

California Dreamin * 5.11a 34
Campbell Soup * 5.10a 265
Camp Stalker ** 5.10d 133
Candy O *** 5.11b 225
Carnival In Hell *** 5.11d 259
Catalina **** 5.10c 79
Celebate Rifle ** 5.10b 137
Central High 5.9 128
Change of Scene *** 5.10a 277
Chaps My Hide ** 5.11c 245
Cheap Lipstick ** 5.7 182
Chemical Warfare 5.11d 85
Chick Flaky *** 5.10c 182
Chick Route * 5.9 269
City Slicker ** 5.10a 139
Clumsy*** 5.12a 65
Combination Lock ** 5.12c 126
Concrete Blonde ** 5.11c 261
Cool Enough ** 5.8 287
Cool To Be You 5.11d/12a 97
Cosgrove Tower 5.10+ 151
Crack in the Armor *** 5.12b 126
Creepy Hollow ** 5.11b 245
Crew of One 5.10b 133
Cromag *** 5.12a 137
Crooked Dick Spire *** 5.9 253
Crossfire *** 5.12a 277
Crowd Pleaser 5.11b/c 44
Crucified 5.11b 196
Cupid's Fever *** 5.8 49
Curly * 5.10d 139
Custom Tailored ** 5.7 225

D

Dance This ** 5.11a 188
Date With Destiny *** 5.12d 261
D&D ** 5.7 251
Deadbolt 5.12c 39
Dead man Walking 5.10a 236
Death Wish *** 5.12d 269
Decaf ** 5.10a 209
Demolition Man 5.10d 196
Descending Opinion ** 5.11a 225

Destination Oblivion 5.9 154
Disconnected ** 5.12c 207
Dita's Play House 5.9+ 148
Dog Ate the Homework ** 5.10a 287
Double Kneebar Ranch **** 5.12b 277
Dr. Know ** 5.10b 182
Drunken Midget Wrestling 5.11a 87
Dry Spell ** 5.9 57

E

Easy Prey ** 5.9 128
Espresso *** 5.10c 209
Evil Offspring *** 5.12c 277

F

Face to Face **** 5.11d 245
Fair Weather Friend ** 5.11d 265
Fantasia **** 5.11a 242
Fine Day ** 5.10a 259
Fire Starter *** 5.13d 255
Flame Thrower ** 5.11c 242
Freakshow **** 5.12a 247
Fred *** 5.9 75
Friendly Fire ** 5.11c 271
From the Ashes 5.10d 196
Fun in the Sun ** 5.9 182
Funny Face *** 5.11a 139
Funny Like A funeral *** 5.12a 261

G

Gallows Pole 5.10c 89
Generous Portions ** 5.10 57
Getaway *** 5.10a 233
Getty-Up ** 5.11a 137
Girl Scout Cookies ** 5.7 288
Goldfinger * 5.10a 182
Gonna Be Just Like Them ** 5.10c 85
Good day Sunshine *** 5.10c 115
Good to be Awake *** 5.11b 188
Green Eggs and Ham ** 5.7 288
Grey Area 5.8 227
Guilt Free ** 5.12b 65
Guilty as Sin ** 5.12b 65
Gun for Hire *** 5.11b 188
Gut Reaction 5.11a 177
Guttermouth * 5.11d 271

H

Hale Bop Tango ** 5.8 197
Hallraker **** 5.12d 124
Hang Daddy ** 5.11b 57
Hangman 5.12a 89
Hateful Little Girl 5.12b 65
Headhunter 5.11b 39
Hero Worship *** 5.11b 126
Hidden Agenda **** 5.11c 139
Hidden Grotto Left 5.9 152
Hidden Grotto Right 5.10a/b 152
Hole In One *** 5.11a 245
Holy Moley *** 5.10a 211

I

Idiots At Happy Hour *** 5.10a 92
Improbable ** 5.11a 277
Inconceivable *** 5.8 154
Indirect Action *** 5.9 199
It Puts the Lotion on its Skin 5.7 148
Ivy Alice ** 5.6 288

J

Jack be Nimble *** 5.9 287
Jug Haul ** 5.9 277

K

Kestrel Dihedral 5.7 149
King of all Media *** 5.11d 177
Kiss 5.10b 236

Index

Korean Wall Route 1 5.7 145
Korean Wall Route 2 5.10 145
Korean Wall Route 3 5.11b 145

L

Lady In Red 5.11c 99
La Fissura 5.9 191
Left Flank ** 5.10a 287
Legion of Evil *** 5.11a 81
Lethal Weapon *** 5.12d 269
Let's Kung Fu ** 5.12c 177
Life of the Party ** 5.11c 35
Life Returns 5.11a 196
Little Jack Horner * 5.6 175
Little Red Book *** 5.10a 204
Little Stiffy *** 5.11c 204
Lock Down ** 5.10c 259
Lost in the Middle **** 5.12b 65
Lost Your Edge 5.11c 141
Love Onsite*** 5.10c 217

M

Macho Insecurity 5.11a 261
Madam X 5.12c 65
Make A Way *** 5.10b 287
Mantling 101 5.10b 227
Marked For Death * 5.11b 269
Master of None **** 5.13b 35
Maynard G. Krebs *** 5.12b 271
Mental Block ** 5.12b 126
Midway *** 5.10d 287
Minutemen Arete **** 5.11d 242
Mojo Nation *** 5.10b 245
Mostly Dead ** 5.8 154
Mr. Toad's Wild Ride ** 5.10c 242
My Bloody Valentine *** 5.10a 49
My China Girl ** 5.9 245
My Side of the Roadside ** 5.7 63

N

n00b Arete 5.7 110

N00b Slab 5.6 59
Nervous Breakdown 5.12a 89
Nickel Slots ** 5.11c 245
Nightstick ** 5.11a 259
No Billy No 5.12a 261
No Use for a Name ** 5.12b 109

O

Offwidth 5.11d 139
Oh Behive 5.11a 57
One Eyed Jack ** 5.10c 133
One More Victim 5.11b 196
On the Fringe ** 5.11d 31
Overkill *** 5.11c 288

P

Pat and Jack ** 5.11b 265
Patty Cake ** 5.12a 265
Pinhead ** 5.10a 235
Poaching Bighorns *** 5.10b 79
Potty Training *** 5.7 249
Powder Puff ** 5.7 182
Power Grab 5.12a/b 89
Problematic ** 5.10b 247
Propaganda * 5.11b 65
Pussy Pie ** 5.9 287

R

Rainbow Drive *** 5.11d 123
Raleigh World 5.10a 233
Rattle the Cattle * 5.7 197
Reaching Rayane *** 5.9 287
Red Devil *** 5.12b 207
Red Headed She Devil 5.10+ 154
Red Hot ** 5.12a 182
Redneck ** 5.8 139
Red Tail Arete ** 5.12a 133
Red Tape 5.10c 97
RepoMan * 5.10b 211
Ride the Wild *** 5.12d 109
Roadside Warrior *** 5.9 63

Rob's Rambunctious Ride ** 5.9 217
Room for Improvement *** 5.10d 188
Roughneck *** 5.11a 137
Route 66 *** 5.9 225
Ryane's Revenge ** 5.10a 188
RyBolski ** 5.8 233

S

Same Same but Different ** 5.10c 217
Sam I Am *** 5.8 288
Sex Dance ** 5.11b 188
Sex Magik ** 5.12c 126
Sex Predator/Deviant *** 5.11b 126
Shaky Start 5.10d 204
Shall Remain Nameless ** 5.11c 245
Shell Shock 5.13b/c 31
She Packs Her Bags for Outer Space * 5.11b 59
Shooting Spree ** 5.11c 271
Short and Sassy ** 5.11b 277
Should be Called Do What? ** 5.10c 211
Shreen ** 5.10b 237
Six Pack ** 5.11d 177
Sky's the Limit ** 5.10b 247
Sluttering ** 5.11a 188
Smooth As Silk ** 5.11b 233
Snafu 5.8 236
Sniper 5.12a/b 31
Snow White *** 5.10d 55
Soft Core ** 5.8 259
Solitary Confinement *** 5.12a 124
Something About Mary *** 5.11b 217
Something borrowed something n00b 5.6 110
Sophie's Choice * 5.10a 190
Sort of Silly * 5.10a 259
Split the Scene * 5.12b 277
Stained Glass ** 5.10a 235
Stemroids ** 5.11a 55
Step Across *** 5.10a 217
Step Right Up 5.8 236
Stop Staring At My Ass ** 5.11b/c 97
Stop the Madness *** 5.12a 204
Story of J ** 5.10a 237
Straight Ahead ** 5.11b 123
Suddenly Susan ** 5.11a 223
Sundowner 5.10c 196
Sunny Up ** 5.9 115
Sunshine Superman * 5.10a 115

T

Taylor Made ** 5.8 223
Technically Inept *** 5.10a 97
The 4 Horsemen **** 5.11a 158
The Action **** 5.13a 156
The Crawl Space ** 5.9 158
The Critic 5.12b 41
The DX 5.13a 150
The Flake ** 5.10a 139
The Hall V-Easy 51
The Last Coyote *** 5.12+ 277
The Low IQ V-Easy 51
The Meat 5.12c 39
The Possibility *** 5.11d 277
The Predator *** 5.12c 126
The Pups Are Doggin' It 5.11a 190
The Raven ** 5.11a 211
The Roundup ** 5.10b 137
The Scene Is Not For Sale *** 5.11a 277
The Snake *** 5.10d 81
The Travesty **** 5.13a 109
They All Look the Same ** 5.11d 188
Third Input * 5.12a 245

Index

This Nazi Shit Won't Do 5.11b 128
Three Giant Steps *** 5.10a 287
Tight Black Vinyl 5.11a 261
Tikiman 5.12b 39
Toe Tag ** 5.8 158
To Infinity and Beyond 5.11b 143
Tommy Thompson Route 5.12a 39
Tough Choices ** 5.10c 213
Toxic Box ** 5.11a 81
Tradliness 5.11c 92
Truculence ** 5.6 288

U

Uncle Funs Basement *** 5.7 154
Under the Gun *** 5.13b 269
Unknown Route 5.10d 204
Unleash the Dragon ** 5.8 288
Use Your Mind *** 5.11a 57

V

Venus Envy ** 5.10a 287
Vertigo ** 5.11a 126
Victoria's Secret *** 5.8 49
Violent Arrest 5.11+ 90
Voodoo Child *** 5.13b 207
Voodoo Lounge *** 5.13a 207
Vortex ** 5.11c 242
Voyeur ** 5.11a 139

W

Waiting For Anarchy *** 5.11b 92
Walk in the Park * 5.8 182
Walk the Talk *** 5.12c 199
Watchtower Direct * 5.11a 156
Welcome to New Jack City *** 5.10a 217
We're A Happy Family * 5.10c 235
Westward Ho * 5.11d 59
What's New Jack *** 5.10c 115
What The...* 5.10a 191
White Flight * 5.7 55
White Head ** 5.9 55
White Out *** 5.10b 55
Whiter Shade of Pale ** 5.6 55
Will Power ** 5.11a 213
Woody 5.9 143
Working Men R Pissed 5.9 199
Wrangler Arete *** 5.10c 233

Y

You Don't Know Jack **** 5.12c 207
You Get What You Deserve *** 5.12d 65
You Just Got Jacked 5.10a 57

Numbers

72 Hour Hold 5.9 199
1964 5.11+ 150
2016 5.11+ 150

THE FACTORY BOULDERING
BUILDING BETTER CLIMBERS

— SO CAL'S PREMIERE BOULDERING GYM —

[
10,000 SQ. FEET OF CLIMBING
250+ BOULDERING PROBLEMS
ALWAYS ADDING NEW CLIMBS
TRAINING EQUIPMENT + FULL GYM
]

714-639-7625
1547 W. Struck Ave Orange, CA 92867
www.thefactorybouldering.com

www.ingramcontent.com/pod-product-compliance
Lightning Source LLC
Chambersburg PA
CBHW062056290426
44110CB00022B/2609